Publish and be damned
www.pabd.com

Angel Wine

Andrew Stilton

Publish and be damned
www.pabd.com

Designed in London, Great Britain, by Adlibbed Limited.
Printed and bound in the UK or the US.

ISBN: 1-905290-65-9

ACKNOWLEDGMENTS

Thanks to Sam for giving up her free time to help with the typing and to Myra for her knowledge of 1980s music and fashion (amazing for one so young).

To Ruth, Lucy and Anna with love.

Chapter 1

For some unaccountable reason, Nigel Troy was humming Sweet's *Wig Wam Bam* as he walked down Corben Road, Islington (neatly swerving to avoid an elderly lady with a walking frame and (incongruously) a sweatshirt bearing the legend *Fancy A FCUK?*), unlocked the door to Number 13 and began to read his one item of post, the inevitable letter from a timeshare company informing him that he and he alone was the lucky winner of their star prize. All he had to do was call an 0898 number (**Calls will be charged at £3 per minute*) and then attend a brief presentation (doubtless at a time and place inconvenient for him), where a cheque for up to one million pounds would be awaiting him.

His brief pleasure was somewhat dissipated when he saw an identical envelope addressed to Amanda, Mrs. A.S.G. Cadogan-Troy - when they married, Amanda had initially refused point blank to assume the monosyllabic Troy in place of the (in her opinion) more patrician surname of Cadogan, but eventually they reached a compromise and became the Cadogan-Troys.

Looking at the particulars of the timeshare complex they were promoting (" a unique development, built in Moorish style but to the highest specifications, with access to three golf courses and within ten minutes' drive of the shops, beaches and nightlife of Marbella") he reflected that, with its twenty-four hours a day, seven days a week office facilities and the "wire-less internet hotspots to enable you to send and receive e-mails via your laptop while you top up your tan and sip an ice cold drink beside the blue waters of our swimming pool" it would be an ideal holiday retreat for Amanda - despite the fact that several years previously she had dismissively written-off the whole of the Costa Del Sol as Shell Suit City.

Nigel was 46, a lecturer in tax law at a London university, a depressing 1960s institution recently given university status (Magdalene College, Hackney, as Amanda unkindly liked to call it).

He was a little taller than average, of slim build, with a shock of fair hair, which was beginning to turn grey, and generally had about him a rather distracted, academic air.

"Unspoilt by progress" was how Amanda often described him.

"Hi, Boss" came the cheery greeting from his son, Matt. "Don't forget that I've invited the lads round tonight to watch the football. Just going to the offie to get some beers. Oh….and Mum is stuck in a meeting as usual."

With that he was gone.

Nigel groaned inwardly at the thought of the house being invaded by Matt's crowd of rugby club friends: Matt was eighteen and, Nigel was a little ashamed to admit, the sort of hale and hearty type that had always made him feel more than a little inadequate at school-and often during his student days, too. Although his son normally treated him with almost exaggerated courtesy and respect, Nigel always sensed something rather condescending in his manner and had to admit that he rarely felt entirely comfortable in Matt's company.

This was not how he had planned his life, he thought later as he ate his meal in the solitary confinement of the study, well away from Matt and his rugby-playing hearties. He was listening to one of his favourite albums, Bob Dylan's *Desire*, which always reminded him of his second term at Cambridge, back in the early spring of 1976. Dylan's distinctive vocals, backed by the beautiful, clear voice of Emmylou Harris and the violin of Scarlett Rivera, always conjured up memories of those wonderful late night coffee and toast sessions with Pete and Roger, when they would talk into the early hours about what, a few years later, the Hitchhiker's Guide To The Galaxy would call Life, The Universe and Everything, together with more weighty matters such as cricket, football and women.

After *Desire*, he played *Blood on the Tracks* - the best ever album of songs about love and loss, he had always thought. As ever, they caused his thoughts to turn to the two great "What Ifs" of his life - Jane, a girl he had met in Dinard in 1973 and Sally, whom he had known for a few months in Cambridge. With Sally, his big regret was ending the relationship (as he subsequently realised) prematurely, while with Jane he had failed conspicuously even to begin it.

Until that trip to Dinard, his interest in the opposite sex had been more theoretical than practical, as evidenced by a piece of paper that he had recently found in his ageing copy of Day of the Triffids and which he re-read as he listened to Dylan singing *If You See Her, Say Hello.*

The World's Most Beautiful Women – Nigel Troy, 6.4.73.
1. *Brigitte Bardot (actress)*
2. *Bobby Gentry (singer)*
3. *Alexandra Bastedo (The Champions)*
4. *Penny ? (Sharon in Please Sir)*
5. *Venus (Fireball XL5)*
6. *Evonne Goolagong (tennis player)*
7. *Clodagh Rogers (singer)*
8. *Eva Reuber-Staier (ex-Miss World)*
9. *Eva? Ava? (Eddie Albert's wife in Green Acres)*
10. *Babs (brunette from Pans People)*

He well remembered compiling that list in between lessons and that the inclusion of Venus had caused a major row with Micky Campbell who was compiling his own list and objected to Venus and to Marina from Stingray. In the end, Nick Wooldridge had brokered a settlement under which Nigel was allowed one puppet (Venus) in return for allowing Micky to include a cartoon character (Daphne from Scooby Doo). The unfortunate Marina was replaced by the nameless actress from Please Sir.

On the back was a further list, which had obviously been compiled at the same time:

Top Ten All-Time Favourite Records-Nigel Troy, 6.4.73
1. *Honky Tonk Women-Rolling Stones*
2. *Girl-Beatles*
3. *Layla-Derek & The Dominoes*
4. *When The Levee Breaks-Led Zeppelin*
5. *Celebration Day-Led Zeppelin*
6. *Silver Machine-Hawkwind*
7. *Livin' Lovin' Maid-Led Zeppelin*
8. *Lay Down-Strawbs*
9. *Paranoid-Black Sabbath*

10. Black Night-Deep Purple

Innocent, carefree, days they seemed now, he thought-and so different from now. Feeling in a reflective mood, he took a sheet of paper and began to draw up a balance sheet to show the state of his life at the age of forty-five:

Nigel Troy - Balance Sheet as at May 2003

Credit	Debit
Professional:	
Trained with top city firm - Admitted as a solicitor in 1981	*Failed to make it to partner or even associate*
University lecturer in tax law	*Third rate uni and it bores me (and my students) senseless*
Personal:	
Attractive and intelligent wife	*Never mind the 3 in Charles' and Diana's marriage-there are 83 people in mine - Amanda, myself and the entire Bodkin Manners Corporate Finance Department*
Two healthy, good-looking and tolerably intelligent children	*My son patronises me and my daughter largely ignores me (but ? loves me)*
Material gains:	
Expensive 5-bedroomed house in smart part of London	*For the price, we could buy a mansion in Dudley (but would I want to live there?)*

Accomplishments:	
Brilliant exponent of air guitar	*Told by charmless harpy at Cambridge that I looked a complete ponce when I played air guitar to Layla on the dance floor.*
	Bestsellers written: none
	Music composed: none
Ways in which I have made the world a better place:	*None*

All in all, he decided, the debits well and truly outweighed the credits. How had it come to this? he asked himself. Back in 1973 I was the golden boy of my school (academically anyway) - the Pupil Most Likely To Succeed. I was going to play football for Wolves and cricket for England and then go on to become a top Q.C, finding time to date Suzi Quatro and Raquel Welch along the way. Winning a scholarship to Cambridge was going to be my passport to fame and fortune. Look at me 30 years on-I'm empty and aching. Whatever happened to those teenage dreams?

Chapter 2

1973 now seemed like a different planet. It was the era of Donny Osmond and David Cassidy and Nigel and his family were living in a pleasant, tree-lined road in Dudley, where he went to a local boys' grammar school, with compulsory Latin, rugby and canings. In those days, the town still had some of its old grandeur, with its wide High Street and thriving market place and the ruined castle on the hill above the zoo.

His father drove an Austin Maxi which was a couple of years old and therefore rusting profusely, while his mother (like all the other mothers at his school) drove a bright orange Datsun Cherry, which had recently replaced the ageing Triumph Herald, with its James Bond bullet holes and the fading *I've Got A Tiger In My Tank* sticker on the rear window. To Nigel's massive relief, as a gesture of supreme generosity, when she sold the Herald she had thrown in the nodding dogs which had graced the rear parcel shelf for some years and which had begun to cause him considerable embarrassment.

By then, the optimism of the sixties had faded and the world seemed to have changed irretrievably, with increasing tension in the Middle East (which culminated later in the year in the Yom Kippur War), daily violence in Northern Ireland and regular hijackings and other acts of terrorism. In Britain it was the era of seemingly incessant strikes, power cuts and shortages (in Dudley, an elderly man had to be taken to hospital with injuries sustained during the stampede that began when a few bags of sugar appeared on the shelves in George Mason).

After sitting his O-levels, he was looking forward to the less restrictive regime of the sixth form but before that to a school trip to Dinard.

It would be the first time he had spent more than the odd night away from his parents and, on the eve of his departure, his mother (this being her post- Galloping Gourmet   but pre-Delia Smith culinary phase) marked the occasion with a special departure Vesta (packet) Paella dinner (rather than the usual boil-in-the-bag cod in non-descript sauce and

Smash instant potato) which she followed with strawberries topped with Angel Delight, while his father (not normally noted for such spontaneous outbursts of generosity) even gave him a football-shaped Soap-on-a-Rope as a leaving present, accompanied by a muttered imprecation about cleanliness being next to godliness.

Later on, though, he had to endure the presence of his parents' friends, Mr and Mrs Woodhead, for one of their fortnightly bridge evenings, which he found an ordeal at the best of times. That night, in particular, it all seemed to be symptomatic of the middle-aged, small town lifestyle that (for ten days anyway) he was about to leave behind and so he skulked away in the peace of his room, listening to John Peel on the radio, until he heard his mother calling him from the foot of the stairs:

"Nigel, darling, could you do me a favour?" Could you ask Mr and Mrs Woodhead whether they'd like tea or coffee and then make it for me? Then you can come and talk to them for a bit."

"Oh, Mum, do I have to?"

"Yes you do. If you are old enough to go off to France on your own, you're old enough to talk nicely to adults."

With bad grace, he went into the living room and scowled at the guests.

"Hello. Do you want tea or coffee?"

"I'd like some more of your father's excellent home brew, please" replied Mr Woodhead with his usual joie de vivre, which never failed to get on Nigel's nerves. "It's very good stuff, Reg. How do you make it?"

"It's easy - you can buy the kits at Boots or Timothy White's. It works out at about six new pence a pint - not bad, is it?"

"Six pence? What's that worth?" asked Mr Woodhead, in the general direction of his wife.

"Just over a shilling" was her almost instant reply. "I don't need my Ready Reckoner any more," she added proudly.

When she had made certain that the assembled company were suitably impressed, she turned her attentions to Nigel."

"Anyway, how are you, Nigel, pet. Are you looking forward to going to France?"

"Yes, thank you, Mrs Woodhead."

"If you're old enough to go to France without your parents, I think you're old enough to call me Norma" she leered, rather suggestively, he thought with a shudder.

He glowered in her direction, then made a dive for the kitchen where he reflected on the irony that the only apparent benefit of reaching the age of consent seemed to be that he was allowed to ply golden oldies with coffee and home-brewed beer and to call them by their Christian names.

Can I be the only sixteen-year old male in the Western Hemisphere, he wondered, who has yet to kiss a girl? Even Dave Such, with the looks of a male Medusa - guaranteed to turn to stone all those who gazed on his ghastly countenance - was rumoured to have been seen necking at the after-show party with the girl who played Bonnie Jean in the local Youth Theatre production of Brigadoon. Still, if there was somebody in the world who fancied Dave, there must be hope for everyone.

He returned to the living room carrying the drinks and Mr. Woodhead beamed at him (a tad patronisingly, Nigel thought).

"How do you think that football team of yours is going to do this season then, Nigel?"

"Okay, I think."

"Did I ever tell you that I used to watch them in the 'fifties, when they used to play Moscow Dynamo and all the other top teams in Europe?"

"Yes, Mr. Woodhead" Nigel replied wearily. "Many times."

"Those were the days-Billy Wright, Bill Slater, Mullen and Hancox on the wing.... Real footballers they were, not like these over-paid Nancy boys nowadays, with their long hair and sideboards. Fancy paying over two hundred thousand pounds for a footballer."

"And in those days they didn't kiss each other when they scored" put in his father gratuitously. "At least that doesn't happen on the cricket field."

"Not yet, anyway" retorted Mr. Woodhead darkly.

" We managed to beat New Zealand but I think we'll struggle to beat the West Indies, don't you, Arthur?"

"I'm sure we will-that Gary Sobers is still a fine player. They're not as good as they were in the days of Weekes, Worrall and Walcott, of course, but they'll still be too strong for us. There's not one of our lot that would have got into a pre-War England side, except maybe Boycott…and Knott, if he'd get his hair cut."

"That bloke Arnold bowled well against New Zealand, mind-floating it round like the Pound, he was."

He was answered by a derisory snort from Mr. Woodhead. "The Pound indeed-I never thought a Conservative Chancellor would make such a mess of the economy. I can remember when there were four Dollars to the Pound and that was that-we knew our place in the world then."

His father drew deeply on his pipe: "The country's going to the dogs, Arthur."

"Too right, Reg - we'll be a communist state in five years."

"With Comrade Wedgwood-Benn as President, no doubt."

"You know what I think? I think we need a period of military rule to bring us all to our senses. That would sort out a few of those bearded weirdoes - either that or a good war."

"That Ted Heath's a lily-livered leftie, if you ask me. More interested in playing with his organ than sorting the country out."

Mr Woodhead sniggered appreciatively. "Nixon's the sort of bloke we need - but looks like he's in trouble with this Watergate affair."

"Makes you wonder what sort of world we're bringing our kids into - no wonder they're all drug addicts, what with all that pop music and Play For Today - and that Monty Python's Circus thing."

The pair fell silent and Nigel, who had switched off at the beginning of the conversation and had spent the last couple of minutes trying to imagine what Suzi Quatro would look like with no clothes on, realised that all the adults were looking at him.

He stood up and smiled at his father.

"Just off on an LSD trip now, then, Dad."

"I beg your pardon" came the shocked reply.

"I said I'm just going to finish packing for my school trip. Goodnight Mr Woodhead… Goodnight, Norma", he added, darting past her at a rate of knots, as he could see her lips beginning to pucker and knew from bitter experience that she was quite capable of demanding a goodbye kiss from him.

Back in his room, he put on *Stairway To Heaven* and reflected on the irony that the only member of the opposite sex who had designs on his lips was a geriatric whose sole *raison d'etre seemed* to be to impress her friends and acquaintances with her grasp of decimalisation, which every moderately intelligent four-year old in the country had understood within minutes. He also vowed then and there that in his middle age he would never bore the next generation with how and why the sporting heroes of his youth were so much better than their modern day counterparts.

But…why should he care? In a few hours he would be away from his parents and their tedious friends - free to sample the local wine, to have some fun with his friends and to find romance with a pretty Breton girl.

The following morning, he made his own way to the school, where the party for France was already assembling, Dave Such and Rick Powis looking like a couple of young peacocks in identical aubergine cords and yellow and blue striped shirts, Nick Woodridge wearing the Afghan coat which his one-time hippy brother had discarded on joining a firm of chartered accountants and nearly everybody else wearing faded Levis or Wranglers and a tie-dye tee-shirt.

There was a cheer as the coach pulled out of the school gates, which was soon replaced by howls of protest when the driver put Radio Two on and turned the volume right up.

"Sacre bleu!" exclaimed Kevin Yardley. Are we going to have to put up with   Peters and Lee all the way to piggin' Calais? "

"We'll have a job - we're crossing over to Cherbourg, *dumbkopf*" yelled Stewart Edwards. Anyway, it'll probably be Max Bygraves next, with *Tulips From Amsterdam.* Or maybe that awful Sandy Shaw song about the Frenchman with the continental kiss."

"Monsieur Does Pong wasn't it called?" asked Nigel. "Anyway, lads, hasn't anyone got a cassette player?"

Eventually Nick Wooldridge produced a rather tinny sounding tape recorder and a group of them clustered round it at the back of the coach and began to yodel along to *Hocus Pocus* and *Sylvia* by Dutch band Focus, just about drowning out Radio Two's offering of *Tie A Yellow Ribbon.*

Once on the boat, Nigel and a group of friends spent most of their time playing cards in the lounge and remained oblivious to the seasickness around them, until Kevin Yardley came in to announce gleefully that Dave Such and Rick Powis had made a new friend. "I think he must be called Hugh" he continued dryly, as they've both spent the last hour leaning over the side and calling 'Hughie, Hughie'. That's what it sounded like, anyway."

Nigel went rushing over to witness his colleagues' discomfort, only to slip on a pile of vomit and fly headlong into an elderly gentleman of military bearing with a voice to match, who snapped "young fool" in response to Nigel's hearty apology. Even at sixteen, Nigel was perceptive enough to realise that, in the man's eyes, his principal crime was his youth rather than his apparent stupidity.

You're an old man, full of bile, he thought. You're bitter because you've wasted all your opportunities and resent the fact that I've still got my whole life ahead of me. He debated whether to articulate these thoughts but in the end contented himself with raising a two-fingered salute - a Harvey Smith, as it was known in those days - in the man's direction. His old road's rapidly ageing, he told himself, while yours is just beginning.

The general bonhomie came to an end when they arrived at their accommodation - a rambling, rather forbidding boarding house called Ker Dumont, on a leafy residential avenue. The weather was grey and miserable and Nigel found himself wishing that he had elected to go on the family holiday to Ibiza instead.

They were greeted by the unsmiling *Maitre d'* with a long list of do's and don'ts in which the don'ts outnumbered the do's by about five to one.

"What do you think the grub will be like?" wondered Nigel aloud to Nick Wooldridge.

"It'll probably be the minced remains of guests who played ball games on the lawn or used more than ten centimetres of water in the bath."

The answer became apparent at dinner time when they were presented with pate de foie which looked remarkably like fish paste, followed by some spindly chicken in some sort of sauce, which was immediately christened Sparrow-Au-Vin - all served by the saturnine proprietor (Norman Bates as he soon came to be known). All in all, the start of the holiday could hardly have been less auspicious.

After a couple of days, however, the gloomy mood was lightened by the arrival at Ker Dumont of a party from a comprehensive school in Shrewsbury, which included a number of eminently nubile third and fourth year girls, prompting Stewart Edwards and Jeremy Prior (normally known as Mungo Jerry) to lead their colleagues in a hearty rendition of *There's Nothing Like A Dame*.

Nigel's attention was soon attracted to one particular girl– she was petite, with long dark hair tied back with a bobble, green eyes, a ready smile and a wardrobe in which everything seemed to be brown except for the flared jeans that she wore all day, normally accompanied by a tank top. In the evening she would   change into a maxi skirt and a brown cheesecloth blouse and, he soon decided, always looked the prettiest of the bunch.

Eventually he steeled himself to make some discrete enquiries about her from Dave Such, who seemed to have ingratiated himself with the girls remarkably quickly.

"Hey, Dave" he muttered in what he thought were suitably confidential tones. "What's the name of the girl over there - the one in the brown top?"

"They're all wearing brown tops, Doris, you fool."

"Okay, okay, she's wearing an orange skirt as well."

"Oh, her? That's Jane."

"Does Rick fancy her? He seems to be talking to her a lot."

"Nah, he's after her friend, the one next to her now, with the skinhead haircut. Heather I think she's called. Taken a fancy to Jane, have you, Doris, you old Casanova, you?"

"Well, she does look rather nice."

"Say no more! Say no more! She's a Wolves fan like yourself, so if her taste in blokes is as bad as her taste in football teams, you should do fine. Know what I mean? Know what I mean? I tell you what - I'll introduce you to her if you'll buy me a packet of Gauloises tomorrow."

"Alright, it's a deal. Just give me a moment to get myself ready... won't take long" he added as he raced up the stairs to his room for some Dutch courage from a bottle of rosé that he had hidden in his case and to apply a little of the Hai Karate aftershave that he had bought in the Duty Free shop on the ferry.

On the way, he decided upon his strategy, which was to come across as warm, humorous and so much more sophisticated than the boys in her class.

Dave was waiting for him and led him over to where Jane was standing among a group of girls.

"Jane, may I introduce you to my good friend Doris, here? He's a fellow Wolves fan - so that makes two of you. Say no more, say no more!"

Jane wrinkled up here nose in the direction of Dave's back, as he turned away and headed off towards the bar. "Is your friend a bit of a weirdo? Does he have to end every sentence with 'say no more'?"

Nigel laughed: "Apparently so. He and Rick - the bloke over there with all the hair on his head - can't carry on a conversation for more than two minutes without it turning into a recital of a Monty Python sketch. We all went to the Edgbaston cricket test last summer and they spent the entire day annoying the Australian team by shouting 'well played, Bruce' every time one of them fielded the ball. I thought Denis Lillee was going to thump them at one point."

He paused.

"Are you a Python freak, Jane?"

"Not really: they're quite funny sometimes but it gets on my nerves when everybody at my school spends all day every Friday doing a re-run of all the sketches from the night before. I prefer the Goodies.

"Anyway, why do they call you Doris?"

He flushed "My name's Nigel Troy but somebody found out that there was an American singer called Doris Troy - she sang backing vocals on *Dark Side Of The Moon*, in fact - and started calling me Doris. I hate it - I used to be called Tempest, after Troy Tempest from Stingray."

"That suits you better: Troy Tempest used to be my hero - him and Steve Zodiac from Fireball XL5 and Ilya in The Man From U.N.C.L.E."

"I used to love Fireball."

"I like Ben Murphy from Alias Smith And Jones now - and the one who plays Trampas in the Virginian."

"Doug McClure?"

"That's him. He's a bit old but he's really good looking."

"I like the Virginian - I always feel that the weekend's started when that comes on. Perhaps that's why I hate Star Trek - because it comes on on a Monday evening and there's four days of school ahead. It used to be the same with the Andy Williams Show."

"Do you like Doctor Who?"

"Not so much now - I used to watch it every week when it first came on and was always wandering round the house holding my nose and saying 'I am a Da-lek. Ex-ter-min-ate.' I'm more interested in the football scores on a Saturday evening nowadays."

"Me too."

"Who's your favourite Wolvers player?"

"Dave Wagstaffe, I think".

This is going so well, he thought-time to impress her with how freaky my language can be.

"Hey, man, that's far out, he's my favourite too. Do you go to many games?"

"I go to most home games: I've got two older brothers and my dad dragged me along with them almost as soon as I could walk."

"Dougan's a great centre forward, isn't he? I went to his home debut - he scored a hat trick against Hull City. What a player."

"I prefer Richards, though. Did you see that goal he score against Burnley in the League Cup?"

"No, it was just my luck that it was one of the nights when we had power cuts because of the miners' strike or whatever it was. I heard it on the radio, though-I was trying to do my homework by candlelight at the same time."

"It was funny during those strikes, wasn't it, when television used to finish at half past ten and then they'd play the National Anthem?"

"My dad loved it-he used to make us stand up while it was playing. Same with the Cup Final."

"I was really glad when Sunderland won the Cup, weren't you?"

"Yeah, I hate Leeds. I couldn't believe that save by Montgomery - you know, the one from Lorimer."

They carried on talking about football for some time, until she changed the subject and asked him what music he liked.

"I'm into Gary Glitter and Little Jimmy Osmond. But Sweet are the very best."

"Are you serious?" she asked with obvious incredulity.

"Absolutely. I really freaked when I first heard *Long Haired Lover From Liverpool* - it was so groovy - but that was before I heard *Blockbuster*. That was definitely the defining moment of my life so far. It was based on a book by John-Paul Sartre, you know."

He paused then laughed at the look on her face. "What a gas! I can't stand any of that teenybopper rubbish. I think I dislike it even more than all that pretentious progressive stuff like Yes and Emerson Lake And Palmer.

"I'm into the heavy stuff - Deep Purple and Led Zeppelin. Robert Plant lives quite near me."

"Do you know him?" He could tell that she was impressed.

"Not very well. He hangs out in an old farmhouse in a place called Blakeshall and I've driven past the house a few times - and I saw him in Dudley one time. It was funny - I don't know whether you have ever been to Dudley but the market place always reminds me of Coronation Street, full of old ladies with their hair in curlers. Groovy! Anyhow, Robert Plant got out of his Mini Moke with all his long blonde hair and I heard one of these old ladies say to her friend 'e looks like the Woyald Man of Bonio.'

"My dad calls it jungle music though. He's into Frank Sinatra and Dean Martin and all that stuff. It's desperate to listen to-a real drag."

"My dad's still mad on the Beatles –he's got all their albums. Some of it's really good actually."

"I like the Beatles - especially Abbey Road. I love that second side when there are all those really short songs one after another - it's really mad. What do you like yourself?"

"I must be the only girl in my class who hasn't got a picture of Donny or David Cassidy on my locker. It's Mott The Hoople I really like - *Honaloochie Boogie* is brilliant. I like David Bowie a lot as well - and Rod Stewart."

"So what's your all-time favourite record?"

"*Paper Plane* by Status Quo, I think."

"And your favourite album?"

"*Ziggy Stardust* - I love that album, especially *Starman*."

"Do you like Strawbs? I think they're really good."

"Weren't they the ones who sang *Part Of The Union*? That was quite good."

21

"Yeah, but they've done much better stuff than that-*Bursting At The Seams* is a great album and the one before, called *Grave New World.*"

"One of my brothers is really into Roxy Music - I think they're very good too. Brian Eno's really good looking, isn't he?"

To his surprise and delight she seemed to be in no particular hurry to finish talking to him - she was very open and friendly and he felt that they had so much in common.

After that first meeting, they seemed to gravitate towards each other every evening and would talk, play cards, or join in a game of *boules*.

From time to time, friends of his would very obviously try to move in on her and chat her up and then he would watch from a distance, racked by jealousy and convinced that she would succumb to their charms but, although she was friendly and approachable towards everybody, he gradually became certain that, hard to believe though it may be, it was he whom she really liked.

One night, the two school parties combined for an impromptu Opportunity Knocks evening, with one of the masters from Nigel's school playing the piano in the corner of the room which Monsieur Norman Bates grandly called the *salon*.

Proceedings began with Dave Such and Rick Powis doing their Pythonesque Silly Walks, followed by a group from Jane's school with *Breaking Up Is Hard To Do* - which had recently been a hit for David Cassidy with the Partridge Family - and then Nick Wooldridge giving an earnest rendition of *San Francisco (Be Sure To Wear Some Flowers In Your Hair)*.

Emboldened by the desire to impress Jane, Nigel leaped up and volunteered to do some impressions, which began (almost inevitably) with Jimmy Cagney repeating "you dirty rat" several times and then moved on to Richard Nixon saying that "there's no whitewash at the White House" and then one or two of the other characters taken off by Mike Yarwood on the nation's television screens every Saturday evening.

The response from the audience was lukewarm at best, until Nick Woodridge suddenly presented him with a beret which he had found in the cloakroom (this being Brittany after all) and which allowed Nigel to do a very passable Frank Spencer and then finish off with Benny Hill (which culminated in his leading everyone in a rousing chorus of *Ernie*

(The Fastest Milkman In The West)).

He received generous applause, but shortly afterwards the event came to a sudden end when Rick Powis reappeared and began to do a very suggestive rendition of Chuck Berry's *My Ding-A-Ling*, prompting Authority to intervene and call a halt to proceedings.

Nigel wandered over to talk to Jane, his face glowing with satisfaction at the success of his performance.

"I'm most impressed, Nigel" she smiled at him. "I thought your Brian Clough was absolutely brilliant - although I'm not sure why he would be going on about 'the pound in your pocket.'"

Nigel's face fell "That was supposed to be Harold Wilson actually" he muttered, provoking a fit of giggles from Jane.

"Oh, Nigel, you are so easy to wind up. It was just like having Mr Wilson in the room with us. Come on: I'll buy you a Coke to celebrate finding out that you're a man of so many parts."

The last day was hot and sunny and both school parties made for the beach, where for the first time he saw her in a swimsuit. They talked for a time about the football season ahead, while Nigel tried to think of a romantic gesture that he might be able to make - to declare his feelings for her and to spirit her away from the gaze of their respective friends. Eventually he had what he thought was a moment of inspiration.

"Would you like a game of table football?" he gestured with his head towards the arcade on the sea front.

"But I don't really like table football, Nigel" she laughed. "I'll tell you what, though, I wouldn't mind going out on a pedalo."

"Your wish is my command" he bowed and a few minutes later his chest was swollen with pride as they pedalled out to sea to (he had no doubt) the envy of all his friends.

"So" he asked, "are you looking forward to going back to England?"

"So-so. It'll be good to see my family, I suppose - and McIlmoyle, of course."

"Who's McIlmoyle" he asked sharply, dreading the response that he was her boyfriend.

"Our dog - he's a retriever cross and he's absolutely beautiful. Dad insisted we call him that after Hugh McIlmoyle, who was the Wolves centre forward at the time. He was transferred a few weeks later, but it was too late to change his name to Dougan by then."

They fell silent for a couple of minutes.

"Have you got a girlfriend?"

"No." Then he added quickly "I have lots of girlfriends but there's nobody special. What about you?"

"No, I haven't got a girlfriend either."

"I mean boyfriends, clever clogs."

"I went out with Dave for a bit last term - you know, the really tall one? - but I finished with him in the end. He's just a mummy's boy."

Unable to think of anything more affectionate to say, he looked towards the beach. "Who are your best friends at school?"

"Heather. And another girl, Alison, who couldn't come on the trip - she had to go on holiday to Barmouth with her parents instead, poor cow. It's funny, they are so different - Heather fancies Skinheads, while Alison only wants to go out with Greasers-but they're both a great laugh. Who's your best friend?"

"Not those two, for sure" replied Nigel pointing to Dave Such and Rick Powis who had also hired a pedalo and were alternately reciting a Monty Python sketch about cannibalism among shipwrecked sailors and making lewd gestures in Nigel's direction whenever Jane's back was turned.

"It's Nick, I think - you know little Nick, the one who always wears Love Beads and was wearing an Afghan coat over his swimming trunks earlier. We're doing the same subjects at A-level - that's if we pass our O-levels, of course. We get the results next week."

"Do you want to go to university?"

"I hope I will - to do law, probably. The school wants me to apply to Oxford or Cambridge."

"I'd like to go too, but I'm not sure if I'm clever enough. I hadn't realised you were such a brain box - are you sure you aren't too clever for me?"

Surely this was the moment for him to declare his affections but the words would not come and all he could do was mutter gruffly "Of course I'm not. I probably won't get in anyway."

"I'm sure you will" she smiled teasingly. "Just do your Brian Clough and they'll be putty in your hands."

presence of mind to reply that he didn't expect the Spanish Inquisition, which inevitably prompted Rick to reply that nobody expected the Spanish Inquisition and by the time he and Dave had exhausted that sketch, they had forgotten all about Nigel's failings and moved on to a verbatim rendition of the demise of the famous Norwegian Blue parrot, leaving Nigel to wallow in his own misery.

Eventually, Nick Wooldridge came and sat on his bed and asked kindly whether he was feeling all right.

"I'm ok, thanks, but...I blew it with Jane tonight. It must have been the romantic equivalent of Jeff Astle missing that open goal against Brazil-now I know how he must have felt."

"It's not that bad, Doris-he had about 100 million people watching him...and he never played for England again, but you're going to have the birds falling at your feet in years to come."

"You reckon?"

"Of course-you're the brightest bloke in the school and you're going to do really well and make lots of money. There's loads of girls who'll want to go out with you-they won't care what you look like."

He never saw Jane again: the next morning they were off to catch the ferry home before Jane and the Shrewsbury contingent were up and that, sadly, was that.

For a long time afterwards he had wondered how different his adolescence might have been if Dave Wagstaffe's shot had hit the crossbar, rather than thundering into the roof of the Arsenal net. In time, though, he came to realise that he would still have fluffed his lines by reminiscing about a Kenny Hibbitt goal or a Jim McCalliog strike - his failure to rise to the occasion had stemmed purely and simply from a youthful lack of nerve, of experience; but that knowledge did not make his disappointment any less.

Chapter 3

Nigel's nostalgic reverie was brought to an abrupt end when his daughter, Galadriel, wandered into the room.

Galadriel was nearly 17, 13 months younger than Matt. She was now at a nearby sixth form college where she had wisely chosen to be known as Ria. The dress code there seemed to be more relaxed than at the all-girls private school that she had previously attended and she had responded by adopting a look -long black dress, dark lipstick, hair dyed jet black and pale make-up – which was apparently known as Gothic, although he preferred to think of it as her Un-Dead phase.

Having previously eschewed the company of the male sex, she had recently had a succession of boyfriends whom he had christened the Ring Wraiths as they all seemed to be bony beyond belief, pale and uninteresting and incapable of articulate speech, the latest being a twenty-year old art student called Kieran who played keyboards in his spare time for a band called The Paranoid Schizoids and whom, to his surprise, he rather liked.

At sixteen, Galadriel seemed to Nigel to be a seething mass of hormones, prone to burst into tears or fly into a screaming rage at the slightest provocation, so much so that Nigel felt the same trepidation when talking to her that he had felt as an eleven year old when addressing a French master of uncertain temper. And yet, ever since she was a very small girl, she had always been the one who was there with a hug or a smile when he needed it and was in many ways the one to whom he felt closest.

"Hi, Dad. Banished to outer darkness again?"

"Afraid so, Ria."

"Cool."

"What have you been up to?"

"Not a lot. Kieran's gig was cancelled at, like, short notice so we just went for a McDonalds and then chilled. How was your day?"

"Usual. You know how it is: half my students seem to have had a total lobotomy, there are a few quite bright ones and the rest-well, the most charitable way of describing them is shades of mediocrity."

"Cool. Still, to be positive, Dad, if these are the people who are going to be advising on, like, tax avoidance in the future, the public coffers should be bulging and they should be able to, like, reduce the tax rates – or give you a pay rise. Mum's completing another of her mega deals is she?"

"Apparently so. You know what it's like – you can't be a real deal maker if you do your deals before midnight".

"Yeah, wicked. Anyway, goodnight Dad."

Reflecting that these desultory exchanges were likely to be the extent of his intercourse with his family for the day, he put on *Dark Side of the Moon*, a record that had long been one of his favourites and always took him back to his teenage years in the 1970s. Nowadays the words of *Time* never failed to strike home:

Then one day you find that ten years have gone behind you
No one told you when to run
You missed the starting gun.

Thirty years had passed behind him since he first heard those words: it was not just that he had missed the starting gun.. he felt that he had never even joined the line-up for the start of the race.

Hanging on in quiet desperation is the English way
The time has gone, the song is over
Thought I'd something more to say.

As a teenager, those particular words always reminded him of childhood visits with his mother to the Johnsons, an elderly couple who had been friends of his grandparents and who lived in a typical inter-Wars semi in a quiet residential road in Dudley. The highlight of their day seemed to be the Archers and Mrs Dale's Diary on the Light Programme. They had a clock which used to chime every quarter of an hour and as Nigel sat with them in the quietness of their living room every chime seemed to be announcing: congratulations - you are now officially another fifteen minutes nearer to death.

In that house, time seemed to pass at a snail's pace, yet his life was now racing by. How come, he wondered, that watching a frame of snooker (inexplicably, a favourite of his mother's ever since the days of Pot Black) felt like an eternity, while the thirty years since he was in Dinard with Jane had passed in the twinkling of an eye? As a boy, his life (and time itself) seemed to be a straight line, occasionally (and at lengthy intervals) broken by a major occasion, such as Christmas, his birthday or going into hospital with chronic constipation. Nowadays, it seemed to be a series of ever-decreasing circles, with birthdays coming upon him with alarming frequency and no obvious way of slowing the process, let alone of reversing it.

One minute, he thought, you are mewling and puking in your mother's arms-and then in no time at all you are eking out your twilight years waiting for the clock to chime. Even worse, you may be in a nursing home or a geriatric ward, with a girl who is young enough to be your great-great-granddaughter saying patronisingly: "Come on, where did we put those teeth of yours?" or "have our bowels opened today then, Nigel?" Perhaps the answer was to spend at least two hours a day watching snooker or videos of Arsenal in the seventies, eighties or nineties, in the hope that this might create the illusion that the passage of time was being slowed.

Sometimes he felt a bitter regret for the years that had drifted by with nothing much to show for them and for the opportunities that had been wasted-the ambitions that he had allowed to be thwarted.

Could it really be thirty years since Dinard?

Whatever had happened to Jane? Would she still remember him? Did she too look back on that dance in Dinard as a seminal moment? A missed opportunity? An old friend of his, Mike Castaldo, now a partner in the same law firm as his wife, had recently been regaling them with some entertaining stories of his own experiences of tracking down old classmates via one of the school reunion websites that he had heard so much about and ever since then Nigel had been wondering whether he might be able to find out what had happened to Jane via one of them.

Not really knowing where to start, he decided to e-mail Mike on what he hoped would not be recognised as the slender pretext that it was.

To: **Mike Castaldo**
From: **Nigel Troy**
Hi, Mike, how're you going?
Was wondering (a) how you are and (b) if you were still working and (c) (if so) how my wife is - we have not had any meaningful communication since the weekend (well, since Christmas actually...)
Best regards.
Nigel

The reply was almost instantaneous

To: **Nigel Troy**
From: **Mike Castaldo**
Hi, Nige, I'm fine thanks and so's Amanda - I heard her rampaging around the department about half an hour ago, kicking the butt of some young associate who had done that which he ought not to have done and/or left undone that which he ought to have done.
We lesser mortals in the property department are a cross that the demi-gods of the corporate finance department have to bear, I am afraid.
She's got a deal which is supposed to complete tonight, I gather, so you can probably expect to see her at breakfast time tomorrow, if you're lucky.
I hope you are well - looks like Wolves might make the play-offs.
Best regards.
Mike

To: **Mike Castaldo**
From: **Nigel Troy**
Thanks for that update, Mike - it's not always easy being married to a demi-god. You aren't the only ones to be treated with Olympian disdain.
Hey, Mike, while I am talking to you, when you and Jan came round to dinner you were telling a great story about how you'd caught up with old schoolfriends via some website: what was that all about?
Nigel

To: *Nigel Troy*
From: *Mike Castaldo*

Was that the story of how I found out that our school bully (real name Ian Lund) is now living in L.A. under the name of Tatiana Summers?

At my school, they had a charming little initiation ceremony known as "bogging" which involved new pupils having their heads flushed down the loo. Just think how much more bearable I would have found that experience as an 11-year old if, when Ian/Tatiana (Bogger-In-Chief) was pushing my head into the pan, I could have seen a vision of him wiggling his way along Hollywood Boulevard in a short skirt and a blonde wig....

If you don't believe me, check him out yourself at www.friendsreunited. com.

Mike

To: *Mike Castaldo*
From: *Nigel Troy*

That's a great story!

There are one or two people I would quite like to track down from schooldays so I may just do that. Thanks, Mike.

Nigel

To: *Nigel Troy*
From: *Mike Castaldo*

Planning to track down old flames, eh?

Be careful you don't do what Charlie Harvey did: he managed to find an ex-girlfriend and they exchanged a few emails, then he sent her one reminiscing about what they used to get up to behind the bike sheds and suggesting they should meet up and rekindle the flame.

It was at that point that she told him the name of her husband - who was one of his major clients!

Mike

To: *Mike Castaldo*
From: *Nigel Troy*

And?

To: Nigel Troy
From: Mike Castaldo
They cut a deal under which she agreed not to tell hubbie if Charlie agreed to reduce hubbie's legal bills by 20%.
I think it's called blackmail but Charlie was more than happy with the arrangement.

To: Mike Castaldo
From: Nigel Troy
Priceless!
Anyhow, I'll let you get on with your work - love to 'Er Indoors if you see her again.
Best regards.
Nigel.

Friends Reunited seemed to be the best way of tracking Jane down but, he wondered, would it be wise to make contact with her after so many years? She would no doubt be a very different person by now-would it be better not to rake up the past?

Nigel agonised for some time but then made his decision: what harm could possibly come from getting in touch with her? He would do it.

Logging on to the Internet, he found the Friends Reunited site but first of all he had to register as member. After doing that, he was offered the chance to add some notes about himself.

He decided that the truth would be far too boring and quickly devised a fictitious CV, which he typed in:

Nigel Troy
After leaving school, I spent some time as a guest of Her Majesty after being found guilty on trumped-up charges of having unlawful carnal knowledge of a gerbil.
On my release, I fronted the seminal punk band the Suppositories but also found time to win Mastermind in 1982 - my specialist subjects being The Magic Roundabout and the lyrics of Showaddywaddy.
On the demise of punk, after appearing in Mother Goose at The Grand Theatre, Basildon, alongside The Krankies and Ed "Stewpot" Stewart, I

was recruited by the CIA to head a counter-espionage unit in Moscow.

After the collapse of the Eastern Bloc, I took time out to lead a British expedition to the summit of K2, and then emigrated to the United States where I am now Senior Pastor of the Mount Clinton Mormon Church in Monicasville, North Dakota.

In my spare time, I am a keen taxidermist and am a regular contributor to the Country Life bridge page.

I have 2 teenage daughters - Vera and Lynn - and a 3 year- old son, Dubya, named after the present incumbent of the White House.

As an after-thought he then added:

One of my (many) wives is Amanda Cadogan, a top London lawyer.

Having done all that, he had to find her school, which he knew had been called St Something-Or-Other's Comprehensive, but by searching against Shrewsbury he soon found it.

He worked out that she would have left school in 1975, 1976 or 1977 and checked the members for those years but to his disappointment there were no Janes. His quest seemed to be over before it had begun, until it occurred to him that one of his own school friends might remember the names of some of the girls so he looked to see who might be listed and was intrigued to find a whole host of names of individuals about whose existence he had (in most cases anyway) long forgotten and with whom he had no particular wish to be reunited.

Martin Abbott
Paul Brooks (Brooksie)
Andrew Carr (Willy)
Charles Cauldwell (Minnie)
Jeremy Edwards (Jez, Eddie)
Peter Goodwin (Blod)
Martin Jones (Jonesie)
Steven Jones (Nathan)
John King (Jason)
David Norman (Spiny)
Stuart Perkins (Dorothy)
Nigel Perry (Noggin, Nog)

Graham Smith (Smithie)
John Southall (Little Plum)
David Such (Cleese)
Clive Wenham (Dead And Gone)

He was momentarily distracted from his quest when he saw the name of Martin Abbott - Abbott had been a rather uninspiring pupil with a distinct lack of social graces, for which he had soon become known to his contemporaries (he had no obvious friends that Nigel could recall) as Blakey after the charmless inspector in On The Buses. Nigel felt a pang of guilt as he remembered that he had been no less merciless in his persecution of the unfortunate Blakey than the rest of his year. Looking back, the boy must have hated every moment of his schooldays.

Putting these thoughts to one side, he worked his way on down the list and for the first (and only) time in his life he was delighted to see Dave Such, whose notes were brief and to the point:

I'm a lumberjack and I'm OK!

To be more precise, I am working in local government and living in Coventry (well, somebody has to). I am OK though!

Hoping fervently that this contact would not lead to his old sparring partner re-emerging in his life on a permanent basis, Nigel sent him a message:

To: **David Such**
From: **Nigel Troy**
Hi, Dave, remember me? Glad to hear you're still around.
Do you keep in touch with Rick?
This may seem an odd request, but I am reliving my adolescence and trying to trace a girl called Jane who was staying at the same dump in Dinard as us.
I know this is a long shot, but can you remember the names of any of those girls?
Best regards.
Nige
In no time, he received a response.
To: **Nigel Troy**

From: **David Such**

Hello, Doris, you old reprobate. Say no more! I do remember Rick taking a fancy to a girl called Heather - a bit of a live wire, from memory.
I do see Rick from time to time-he's as crazy and as ugly as ever.
Hope you are well and OK - still in the Big Smoke?
Dave

To: **David Such**
From: **Nigel Troy**

Thanks, Dave, I will try and check her out.
I am in good form, thanks-you know how it is at our time of life! I can't complain but sometimes I still do.
Great thing about living in London is that it is 25 years or more since anyone called me Doris.
Best regards-and keep looking on the bright side of life!
Nigel (nee Doris...).
PS: Did you see Blakey's name on the Friend Reunited site?
Whatever would give someone like him the urge to be reunited with his tormentors 30 years on?

To: **Nigel Troy**
From: **Dave Such**

Have a look at what he says about himself!!
Intrigued, Nigel clicked on the notes that Blakey had put onto the site
As you all told me, I was a bit of a nerd so I went into computers after leaving school. I went on to set up my own recruitment consultancy for IT specialists and sold it 5 years ago for £22m. Now semi-retired and spending half the year in the Bahamas. I think I can safely say that I have made more money than the lot of you put together.

While half admiring Blakey for making the point, Nigel felt rather sorry that even after 30 years he had clearly not contrived to acquire the grace for making it in a more subtle way.

His quest though was to find Jane rather than to be reunited with Blakey so he turned back to her school list.

Looking through the names, he found a Heather Crowle who had left in 1975 and, feeling like a paedophile (until he remember that this Heather would be about forty four now), he checked her details.

Separated (thankfully!). Living in Newtown, Powys and working in retail management (OK! I work on the checkout at Spar)

Realising that this was probably the best chance of finding Jane, Nigel composed what he hoped was a suitably nonchalant e-mail to Heather.

Dear Heather

Sorry for troubling you but I am trying to track down a girl from your school called Jane whom I met when she was on a school trip to Dinard in 1973.

I seem to remember that she had a good friend called Heather and wondered if this might be you.

Regards.

Nigel Troy

With some trepidation he clicked "Send" and a few moments later received an e-mail from the site operators wishing him success in his attempts to be reunited with Heather.

To his amazement, within half an hour he had a reply from her:

To: Nigel Troy
From: Heather Crowle
Hi, Nigel.

How clever you are to have remembered me!! Yes, I was Jane's bestest friend at school and we were both on the Dinard trip.

I am afraid that I lost touch with Jane a few years ago – We went on holiday to Corfu (bet you didn't know you were talking to Miss Ipsos Wet T-Shirt 1981!!!) and she ended up marrying some bloke she met out there. Last thing I heard, they were running a taverna. Growing old disgracefully, I have no doubt-like me (given half a chance anyway!!).

Strangely we often used to talk about that holiday in Dinard: Jane took a fancy to some complete geek and virtually threw herself at him but all he wanted to do was talk about the Wolves!! We decided he must have been gay!! We did laugh about that for years afterwards!

Good to hear from you - do e-mail me some more!

Luv Heather

Nigel felt the humiliation of the whole episode surge over him afresh – all those years he had fondly imagined that Jane might be wondering what if things had worked out between them, whereas in reality he had obviously been written off as a geek of doubtful sexuality. Inevitably, he did what he had always done at such times over the last thirty years – he put on Led Zeppelin and played *When the Levee Breaks* at full volume. Feeling vaguely purged after that, but still cursing his youthful lack of confidence and feeling a renewed (and totally unjustified) hatred of his former hero, Dave Wagstaffe, he summoned up the grace for a further exchange of e-mails with Heather.

To: **Heather Crowle**
From: **Nigel Troy**
Thanks for letting me know about Jane. I wonder who the geek was! Are you a keen Wolves fan too?
Nigel

To: **Nigel Troy**
From: **Heather Crowle**
No, Nigel, I hate football - not an outdoor girl at all. I prefer indoor fun…
Heather

To: **Heather Crowle**
From: **Nigel Troy**
Most of my activities seem to be indoors these days too, I am afraid - reading and listening to music, mainly. Have you worked at Spar long?
Nigel

To: **Nigel Troy**
From: **Heather Crowle**
No, only been at Spar since Kylie-Shania was born. Before then I had been working for a few years as an auxiliary nurse.
I like the caring professions - I am quite touchy-feely, me. Very tactile, actually, Nigel!!
Tell me, what star sign are you?

Heather
From: **Nigel Troy**

To: **Heather Crowle**
Libra, apparently.
N

To: **Nigel Troy**
From: Heather Crowle
Mmmm! I am a Scorpio - passionate and creative! And Scorpios and Librans are supposed to be dynamite together!!
It gets very lonely for a girl up here in Newtown - why not come up and see me sometime??!!
Love Heather
xxx

To: **Heather Crowle**
From: Nigel Troy
Heather, yes, I will certainly look you up next time I am passing through Powys.
Nigel

To: **Nigel Troy**
From: **Heather Crowle**
Please do!!
Oh well, time for bed now. I'd better go and get ready - just a dab of scent here and there!!
Sweet dreams!!!
Heather
xxx

Chapter 4

He got up at about seven o'clock just in time to meet Amanda coming home, after her completion meeting.

"Hi, Nigel, everything all right?" she asked, giving him a perfunctory kiss on the cheek.

Amanda was a corporate finance partner at Bodkin Manners, one of the leading City of London law firms. They had met when Nigel was a young solicitor there - widely seen as a rising star in the firm's tax department and on a fast track to partnership - and she was a trainee.

"Did you complete your deal?" he enquired tentatively.

"No, prat of a lawyer on the other side came up with a potential deal-breaker at the last minute. Something arising out of their due diligence work – we've taken it off line and hopefully the VCs will get it sorted today."

The phone rang and Nigel answered it:

"Hello, Nigel" said a cheery voice at the other end. "How's life among the dreaming spires? Ha! Ha!"

"Oh, hello, James, do you want Amanda?"

"Yes please - bit of a problem on a deal we've been working on. I've managed to sort it out but thought I had better bring Amanda up to speed."

James was one of Amanda's assistants, a young man in his late twenties and seen very much as One To Watch for the future. "Clubbable" summed him up - he was bright, intelligent, witty, charming and universally liked and respected by colleagues and clients alike. Nigel could not stand him.

Amanda had two assistants - James and an expatriate Australian called Greg - whom Nigel always thought of as Bill and Ben as they were forever squabbling with each other in their eagerness to impress her. At the moment, James' star was in the ascendancy, as Amanda was highly impressed by his commitment to the job - which he demonstrated by phoning her very late at night and very early in the morning to make sure that she knew that he was a 24/7 man.

Nigel silently handed the phone to Amanda and soon she and James were discussing the intricacies of some obscure part of the Companies Act.

"If only there were more young lawyers like him," she commented when she had put the phone down. "A lot of them seem dead from the neck upwards these days. Anyhow, I've got to be back for a meeting at eleven, so I'm going to have a quick shower and change. See you later, Nigel."

That was what passed for a conversation these days, he reflected – how could he compete with the world of high finance?

As he did not have any commitments at the University that morning, he decided to have a leisurely start to the day, so he made himself a coffee and then put on another Bob Dylan CD. After the disappointment with Jane, he began to think of the second What If? of his life - the girl from 1977, half way through his second year at Cambridge. *Mama You Been On My Mind* always reminded him of Sally - it seemed to sum up his feelings for her perfectly. Time and again she would come to his mind and he would wonder how different his life might have been if only....

Chapter 5

Cambridge had been wonderful fun. He went up in the autumn of 1975 and it was with a wonderful sense of freedom that he realised that there was nobody there who knew anything about him from the past and that never again would he be known as Doris.

His father's Daily Express had given the impression that Britain's universities had long since been over-run by hordes of wild-eyed young undergraduates who, when they were not high on pot (as it was then known) or L.S.D., were waving copies of Chairman Mao's Little Red Book and taking part in violent demonstrations against (in the eyes of the Express) moderate, sensible regimes such as those of Pinochet in Chile and the Greek Colonels.

The truth (to his mild disappointment) turned out to be rather different: the most flourishing political group was the Conservative Association; by far the most popular mind-altering substance was Abbot Ale and the principal hate figure of the time was not some foreign despot but the England football manager, Don Revie, under whose authority any flickering glimpse of flare was immediately extinguished and a hard-fought victory against the likes of Tenerife or Baffin Island came to be seen as a national triumph.

The atmosphere of the place was far-removed from that of his school with its innumerable rules and iron discipline but it was a regime into which he settled very quickly and very easily.

He and Roger had rooms on the same landing and they became firm friends from the outset. Within a couple of days they had got to know Pete who always seemed to be propping up the college bar and the three of them had been inseparable for the rest of their time at college. Although they were very different in background – Roger a public schoolboy from Kent, Pete a grammar school boy from Derby – they were undoubtedly kindred spirits.

The only disappointment with Cambridge was that the ratio of male to female students was about five to one , which meant that girls were in rather short supply, especially as his own college, Trinity Hall, was (until his final year) male only, with the result that there was a phenomenal amount of testosterone contained within the courts and quadrangles of that ancient and hallowed institution.

The most likely place to meet girls was seen to be the Union Society disco which took place every Saturday night but, sadly, those evenings always followed a similar pattern: stand around watching the few girls there dancing round their handbags to *Honky Tonk Women, Spirit In The Sky* and *Born To Be Wild*, then adjourn for a few pints of Adnams and Match of the Day, followed by coffee, toast and Dylan.

By his second year, however, trips to the Union Society become less frequent as there seemed to be a party most Saturday nights which he and his friends would attend with high hopes and three bottles of Hirondelle and it was at one of these parties that he met Sally, who was then in the sixth form at a local convent school.

The early part of that particular evening had always stuck in his memory because they had decided to push the boat out and dine at the Varsity Restaurant, where Nigel (as was his wont) began to complain about his complete lack of success with the female population of Cambridge.

Earlier in the term he had developed what he called the Ugly Sister Technique, which involved spotting an attractive girl with a plain friend and then asking the plain one to dance, on the basis that she was likely to be grateful to be asked and so more likely to accept, but that strategy had borne as little fruit as the more conventional one.

"All that's happened" he lamented sadly, "is that I seem to have been turned down by all the plainest women in this august seat of learning. My ego is in tatters."

Roger, who professed to be rather more worldly wise in such matters, gave him an avuncular smile.

"I hate to say this, Nigel, but do you think that your poor striking rate might have something to do with the fact that you have a certain.... how shall I put it... lack of sartorial elegance?"

"What makes you say that?"

"Well, ever since we've been here your pulling gear has consisted of that delightful brown-and-mauve-patterned Littlewoods jumper that you always wear over one of your fine collection of nylon shirts. Forgive me for saying so but I can't help noticing a tendency to wear the same one several days running and even your usual lashings of Brut aftershave can't disguise the fact that nylon is an artificial fibre which can get a bit hot and sticky in a crowded room."

"Are you trying to tell me I smell?" retorted Nigel, crossly.

"Of course not, but more frequent changes of clothing might prove to be productive."

Although mildly stung by his friend's words, he had to admit that his personal hygiene might not have been all that it should - he never bathed or showered more than once a fortnight and, come to think of it, he only changed his socks and Y-fronts on a weekly basis, at best.

"First impressions " put in Pete, dogmatically "are everything. The way I look at it is that you get to first base when you ask a girl to dance and she says 'yes'; second base is if she lets you buy her a drink..."

"No", interrupted Nigel. "Second base is if she stays with you after the first dance - that's when they normally say 'thank you' and go back to join their friends."

"Okay, so being allowed to buy her a drink is third base, while a slow dance is fourth base."

"Dead right" nodded Nigel, thinking of the number of evenings when the slow records had begun and suddenly everybody in the room seemed to have paired off, leaving him on his own - like a teenage equivalent of musical chairs, he often thought, except that the mad scramble commenced when the music began rather than when it stopped.

Even worse was the moment when the lights went back on to reveal the girl he had been admiring from a distance all evening locked in a passionate embrace with some Neanderthal rugby player... or, as had happened on one or two occasions, with Roger. He winced at the memories.

"What comes after that, anyway?" he asked.

"A home run, hopefully" laughed Roger. "Come on, you two - time to stop theorising and put some of it into practice."

When they arrived at the party, Nigel's eyes soon hit upon a group of girls dancing together, who seemed to be unattached - and in particular upon a petite girl with brown hair and pretty, elfin features.

He watched her surreptitiously for a while before taking advantage of Roger's absence at the bar to canvas Pete's opinion.

"Pete, what do you reckon to the girl over there, with the red and white neckerchief thing?"

"Pretty fit, mate - can't imagine she'd be interested in the likes of you. If you fancy her, though... get stuck in".

"Do you fancy asking one of her friends to dance?"

"Nah, I've got my eye on that blonde standing by the bar - she's a friend of Tim's girlfriend, apparently. You'll have to go and work your charm on your own."

Not wanting to lose face with his friend, at the start of the next record, Nigel went over and asked her to dance, with his usual trepidation (what his Latin teacher at school used to call A Question Expecting The Answer No).

To his pleasant surprise, she smiled shyly and nodded and they began to dance together, while he desperately rehearsed various chat-up lines in his head, before coming out with a rather lame:

"I'm Nigel."

She smiled again and he noticed that she had lovely green eyes.

"Hello, Nigel, I'm Sally. Is this your college?"

"Yeah. I'm in my second year, doing law. But I don't live in college - I share a house with some friends in Bateman Street."

"Bateman Street must be where it's all happening - I'm at the convent there, in the lower sixth."

"So what brings you here?"

"My friend, Maria, is going out with Ian Dobson and he asked her to bring along some dames. So... here I am."

He struggled to think of something sparkling and witty to say before blurting out "you're terminally pretty", which brought a teasing smile to her face.

"Thank you. Am I supposed to tell you that you're brutally handsome?"

He felt disconcerted by her unusual blend of shyness and poise - somehow she seemed to be enjoying a private joke at his expense.

"Not unless that's what you think."

She laughed. "Try Listening to *Life In The Fast Lane* a bit more carefully - but I'm sure you are, anyway."

A little thrown by that comment, he covered up his embarrassment by offering to buy her a drink and then they stood at the bar and talked as best they could above the noise of the disco.

"So, what sort of music do you like?"

"I was brought up on classical music and that's what I listen to the most - but I love the Eagles and Abba. What about you?"

"I'm into Bob Dylan and Led Zeppelin - Robert Plant lives near me. And I'm a big Strawbs fan. Do you live in Cambridge?"

We live on Jesus Green: my dad's a Fellow of Caius and lecturers in Mediaeval History. Where are you from?"

"A place called Dudley, in, er, Worcestershire. You won't have heard of it."

"I have - I'm sure they filmed It's A Knockout there once. My mum hates the programme, but it's quite good fun."

"What else do you like?"

"I love The Good Life and Fawlty Towers. I think John Cleese is brilliant."

They carried on talking and, as he had done four years previously in Dinard, he found himself waiting impatiently for the disc jockey to announce that it was time to slow things down a little - and so it was with some excitement that he eventually recognised the opening bars of *They Shoot Horses Don't They?* by a group called Racing Cars.

"Would you like to dance to this?" he asked thickly - and then she had her arms round his neck and they smooched, while he rehearsed how he was going to avoid a repeat of the kiss-that-never-was with Jane. As he did so, he tried surreptitiously to catch his breath on the back of his hand to make sure that it was as sweet and fresh as it should be-normally, he would swallow a mouthful of toothpaste before going to a party or a disco but the trip to the Varsity had made that impossible.

This time his nerve held and they kissed as the record ended and then spent the rest of the evening in what seemed to him like one long embrace, until proceedings concluded (incongruously) with Peter Cooke and Dudley Moore's *Goodbye-ee.*

He walked her home and then they kissed again at the gate.

"Would you be free tomorrow night, by any chance?" he enquired hopefully.

"I'm sure I would: what time?"

"About 8 o'clock? Would you like to come and see where we live?"

She nodded. "I'd like that, even if it sounds like it's a bit too near to my school for comfort. What number is it?"

"Fifty one."

"Fifty one Bateman Street. Fifty one Bateman Street. I won't forget that - see you tomorrow. Night, night. Sweet dreams."

She kissed him quickly and then disappeared into the garden, leaving Nigel to walk home in a state of complete euphoria.

The next day (a Sunday) he devoted to creating the right impression and ambience for Sally's visit. He had a bath and washed his hair, despite the fact that he had already done so a week or two previously, doused himself liberally with Brut anti-perspirant, changed his socks for the occasion and (in a triumph of hope over expectation) even put on a clean pair of Y-fronts.

In addition to his jeans, he decided to wear an orange (nylon) casual shirt, with the top couple of buttons left open to show the emerging hairs on his chest.

Then came the question of the music that he was going to play: after considering and rejecting 10cc's *The Original Soundtrack* and *Frampton Comes Alive,* he plumped for Eric Clapton and *461 Ocean Boulevard.* The coup de grace, however, was to be the Seduction Tape that he had compiled the previous summer and which he thought that she would be powerless to resist.

He still remembered the running order: the tape began with *Loving You* by Minnie Ripperton and continued with songs like *A Little Bit More* by Dr. Hook and *Make It With You* by Bread, concluding with *Let's Spend The Night Together* by the Rolling Stones and (originally) Dylan's *Lay Lady Lay.* However, in an inspired moment that afternoon, he taped over it with Eric Clapton's *Lay Down Sally* – an attention to detail, which he considered masterful and which, he was sure, would sweep her off her feet.

He could also recall the excitement that he felt that Sunday and the way that it was suffused with an exquisite sense of anticipation. While he was in the bath he had listened to the Top 20 on the radio (number one was *Don't Cry For Me Argentina,* he remembered) and read the sports section of the Observer. Wolves had notched up a famous victory over Liverpool the day before, the days were lengthening and from outside he could hear the birds for the first time in months as well as the occasional sound of a train in the distance - all this and Sally too, he thought to himself smugly.

She arrived on her bicycle, looking demure in a pair of jeans and a round-necked jumper and they sat on the small sofa and kissed for several minutes.

"Say something" she whispered eventually, drawing away from him. "Talk to me."

Nigel frowned a little- kissing was much more enjoyable and much easier than having to make conversation.

"Have you got any brothers or sisters?" was his (rather forced) response.

"I've got an older brother, Patrick, and a younger sister, Bernadette, who is in her third year at the convent. What about you?"

"Just one brother, Simon, who is fifteen."

"Are you enjoying Cambridge?"

"It's wonderful. I found school really dull and restrictive - by the end anyway - and I love the freedom here. There's no one to make you do any work - it's up to you, you can doss around all year if you want to, you just don't get a degree at the end of it.

"I've made some great friends too - I hang around with a couple of reprobates called Pete and Roger most of the time and we do the normal student things. We're planning to go youth hostelling round Europe together in the summer."

Sally's eyes lit up. "That sounds fab. Where do you want to go?"

"Italy and France mainly - but we might get the boat over to Greece and work our way back from there. We haven't really decided yet."

"You must go to Florence: it's got to be the most wonderful city in the world. Paris is pretty amazing too, but I like Florence more."

"Have you travelled a lot?"

"Quite a lot, with my parents. We've been to France loads of times and to Italy. My dad gets invited to various places to lecture so we've been with him to Berlin and Geneva - and to the States as well. Oh, and I went to Vienna last year with the youth orchestra - did I tell you that I play the cello?"

They sounded a civilised family, he thought - somehow, he rather doubted whether Sally's mother would ever have a nodding dog in the window of her car. In fact, she was far more likely to cycle everywhere on a beaten-up old wreck of a bike, with a basket on the front.

"I don't play any musical instruments, I'm afraid. I wish I did - I'd love to play guitar like Jimmy Page or Duane Allman.... or even play drums like Ginger Baker. I play a bit of sport though - squash in the winter and cricket in the summer and I turn out for the college third eleven at football. Do you play anything?"

"We have to play hockey and netball at school, but the only game I really like is tennis. My brother is a football fanatic though - he's very excited because Cambridge United could get promoted to the third division, whatever that means. I support Arsenal, much to his disgust."

Nigel's face clouded over. "It could be worse, I suppose - it could be Leeds. But why Arsenal?"

She laughed. "Patrick always used to make us watch a programme on telly called Quizball and I used to fancy someone called Peter Marinello, who played for Arsenal, apparently. Does he still play for them?"

"No. He was far too skilful, so they sold him years ago." He shook his head. "Arsenal, eh? You'll be telling me you were a Bay City Rollers fan next."

"Well, now you come to mention it.... A couple of years ago you'd have seen me running through the Lion Yard after school, in my tartan trews, singing 'R.O.L.L.E.R.S, Bay City Rollers are the best'."

She suddenly gave what he thought was a surprisingly unlady-like laugh.

"You should see the look on your face: I couldn't stand them - do give me some credit. I was heavily into Mud though... Don't worry, only joking."

He broke off the conversation for a long, lingering kiss and then decided that at last it was time to put on his Seduction Tape; they carried on kissing and then during *Je T'Aime* he made a clumsy lunge with his hand inside her jumper, to which her response was to remove it gently, smile at him and say "I'm not that sort of girl".

Despite his disappointment, he had the presence of mind to reply that he was not that sort of boy either and afterward he had to admit that he had felt some relief as it was normally at that point that television plays faded out and he was not entirely sure of what happened between then and the point where the girl was walking round a bedroom with a sheet covering the parts of her anatomy that he really wanted to see.

They met again a few evenings later and went to meet Pete and Roger at the Alma Brewery where there was live rock music. Sally drank orange juice and seemed to get on well with his friends from the outset, which augured well for the future.

"So, Sally" asked Roger, eventually, in a tone which caused Nigel's heart to sink, "has Nigel told you all about his sordid past yet?"

She smiled gently. "No, I've been spared that so far: is there anything I should know?"

Roger shrugged his shoulders. "It's hard to know where to start-there's so much to tell, isn't there, Pete?"

"It's difficult to imagine how so much depravity could have been crammed into such a young life," agreed Pete solemnly. "Remember the end-of-year disco last summer?"

"I don't think anyone who was there will ever forget it, Pete. Do you want to tell the lady the story?"

"No, you tell her, Rog-I couldn't bring myself to describe such disgraceful scenes."

"Well, here goes, then. On the last night of the summer term, Sally, the college held a disco on the lawn in the Latham Court, down by the river. Normally, it's easier to get an audience with the Pope than to be allowed to walk on the college grass, so it was a memorable occasion and we were all soon…shall we say…in very high spirits.

"Unfortunately, though, there were very few girls and young Nigel here began to get distinctly bored once those that were there had refuse to dance with him and he had Rocked Around The Clock on his tod a few times, so he suddenly announced that he was going for a dip. Next thing, he'd gone out of the gate, disrobed on Garret Hostel Bridge, climbed over the railings and plunged into the academic waters of the Cam."

"Meanwhile," interjected Pete "a friend of ours, Bill Northwick, was sitting on the wall by the river with a beautiful girl he had been wooing all term; she was gazing into his eyes, their lips were about to meet...."

"And then she realized that the silvery orb above the water was not the moon but...the streetlight reflecting off N. Troy's left buttock."

"His right buttock mercifully being enveloped in darkness" added Pete. "And there ended the romance."

"Good job the fish weren't rising to take the worm, eh, Nigel?"

"My friends have never been ones to allow the truth to get in the way of a good story" laughed Nigel, good-humouredly. "I am prepared to admit that I did go for a swim that night but I climbed into the water down the steps by where the college punts are moored and I kept my jeans on throughout. And, anyway, Bill is still going out with that girl."

"That is true, Nigel. She obviously took one look at your naked body and decided that Bill wasn't quite so repulsive after all."

"Whatever the truth of the matter" laughed Sally "I'm glad you didn't decide to round off the party on Saturday night by doing a spot of skinny-dipping."

"I'm far too much of a gentleman, despite what my so-called friends are telling you.

"Anyway, I was wondering if Pete might care to tell you about his own romantic encounter at the party."

"Yeah, go on, Pete" guffawed Roger. "This is a classic."

"If I must" groaned Pete, putting on a pained expression. "You see, Sally, while Nigel was falling for your charms, I was captivated by a rather nubile young blonde who, I was reliable informed by Roger here and by our host, was called Linda and hailed from Derby-which is where I come from.

"So...I asked her to dance and then tried to talk to her about Derby County and what a great player Kevin Hector was, about ATV and Midlands Parade and life in Derby generally...but got zero response and eventually gave up the ghost and went off to watch the football in disgust.

"When I got back to Bateman Street I was bemoaning this lady's lack of personality to my friends and, with great mirth, Roger informed me that she was Norwegian and couldn't speak a word of English. Cheers, friends!"

"So if you've got any nice classmates who would like nothing better than whiling away the long winter evenings talking about Roy MacFarland and great matches at the Baseball Ground, Pete's your man" laughed Roger.

"I'll bear that in mind" she smiled and then looked at her watch. "I'd better be getting home, I'm afraid. It's been lovely meeting you both."

Nigel walked back with her to Bateman Street where she had left her bicycle and they kissed each other good night.

"I do apologise for my friends, Sally."

"Don't be silly-I've had a great time. I think your friends are super-real characters aren't they?"

"Can I see you again soon?"

"Of course-maybe Friday or Saturday? You've got my number, haven't you? Give me a ring. Night night."

"What do you think then, guys?" he asked Peter and Roger when he rejoined them, which prompted them to reply in the Fall-And-Rise-Of-Reginald-Perrin-Speak that had become their equivalent to Dave Such and Rick Powis's Monty Python sketches of a few years previously.

"Great."

"Super."

"Far too nice for a reprobate like you."

"A big improvement on the gargoyles you normally seem to attract."

"I didn't get where I am today without recognising a gargoyle when I see one."

"Come on, then, Nige" asked Roger, breaking into Private Eye catchphrases, "is this the start of an ongoing man-and-woman situation?" while Pete, with less subtlety, asked whether conversations had "taken a Ugandan turn" (a favourite Private Eye expression of the time, originating from an occasion when a couple emerged from a bedroom at a party, announcing that they had been in there "discussing Uganda"). Nigel just sat smiling smugly, congratulating himself on the fact that at last he had contrived to find a girlfriend.

For the rest of term they saw each other two or three times a week – normally in the Alma or the Panton Arms with Pete and Roger in attendance but, at the end of term, in a rare outpouring of romance and sophistication, he took her to the Berni Inn for an intimate Scampi-in-the-Basket followed by the ubiquitous Black Forest Gateau. His abiding memory of that evening was that the background music consisted of orchestrated versions of Demis Roussos' greatest hits, played continually on eight-track cartridge, which meant that by the end of the evening they had heard it from beginning to end several times over.

Despite that, they had a good time, with a lot of laughs and he thought fondly of the evening during the Easter vacation and found himself counting the days until he saw her again.

One Saturday at the start of the summer term they cycled out to Houghton Mill and spent a day there which, in his memory was absolutely idyllic – the weather was glorious and they went punting on the river and then walked in the meadows, before lying together in the long grass, looking up at the vast vault of the Cambridgeshire sky, talking and kissing.

"I love days like this," she sighed eventually, sitting up and looking around her. "The leaves are so pale and delicate, the cherry trees are in blossom- the whole world seems fresh and new, doesn't it?"

"Oh, absolutely" he replied, gazing round quickly to see what she was on about. "It's the company that makes it, though, Sally" he went on before adding, with some (but not total) sincerity: "It's wonderful just being together, isn't it?"

"That's the most romantic thing you've ever said to me, Nigel" she smiled, prompting a sudden rush of affection for her, which would have been the cue for him to profess undying love for her, had he not suddenly remembered Roger's counsel of the night before: "Whatever you do, Nigel, don't get all sentimental and tell her you love her - it can only end in tears."

Instead, his conversation turned to more pressing matters: "Shall we go to that pub in Houghton in a bit - the Jolly Butchers was it? - it looked like they did good basket meals?"

She nodded: "that would be fine. I can't say I'm looking forward to the cycle back though."

"Me neither, but let's forget about it for a bit."

"Good thinking, Batman."

"What's that saying, Sally? 'My cup of happiness truly runneth over.' Lovely surroundings, the warmth of the sun, a lovely girl and, to cap it all, unlike most of the rest of the population of Great Britain we're going to miss the Eurovision Song Contest. Have you heard our entry? It's called *Rock Bottom*, which just about sums it up - although I must admit that Lynsey de Paul is pretty nubile."

Sally laughed. "I have to say that even a ten mile cycle ride home is more appealing than an evening watching Katie Boyle straining to hear a disembodied voice going 'Allemagne un point, Luxembourg nul points.' Although, in defence of Eurovision, it used to be about the only night in the year when we were allowed to stay up after ten o'clock."

"I obviously had a less regimented childhood than you, then, because my brother and I were allowed to stay up to watch the Miss World contest as well. Your parents are pretty cool now, though, letting you go out carousing night after night with your older man."

"They can put up with the carousing but caressing might worry them a bit more - come on, let's go and watch the boats go through the lock."

Despite the fun and romance of that day, however, as the end of term approached, Nigel began seriously to question whether he wanted the relationship to continue over the long summer vacation and into the new academic year. Somehow, the inevitable visits to each others' homes suggested a degree of permanence that he was not sure that he wanted and, less philosophically, he had received intelligence in letters from his brother that Dave Such's sister, Debbie, had taken rather a shine to him over the Easter vacation -Debbie had the reputation of being rather more "accommodating" (as he politely put it to himself) than he had found Sally to be.

He spent some time agonising over whether he should bring the relationship with Sally to an end and (if so) how and when and eventually sought the counsel of Pete, whom he believed to be more experienced in such things but whose approach he guessed might be rather less Machievellian and hurtful than Roger's.

"There's no easy way, Nige" was his advice. "You've just got to be straight with her and tell her you don't want to go out with her any more. You've got to accept that she's likely to be upset but if you're sure you want to end it, then do it sooner rather than later. Sometimes you've got to be cruel to be kind.

"It seems a shame, though, mate - she's a lovely girl. But it's your life, not mine."

Eventually, on the evening of the Queen's Silver Jubilee - a grey and miserable day in the last week of term – he managed to blurt out the lines that he had been rehearsing for some days:

"Er, you know, Sally, it's coming to the end of term and may be it's best we, you know, stopped seeing each other... Not sure I want to get too serious."

He had expected tears and recriminations - or at least some discussion - but she just replied quietly "I suppose you're right, goodbye then," kissed him quickly on the cheek and left, leaving Nigel elated at his bloodless coup and at the thought of the Summer of Lust ahead.

As soon as he got back to Dudley, he called Debbie and fixed a date with her for the first Saturday night of the vacation.

They drove off to a country pub and he was impressed by how sophisticated she had become over the last few months – she drank a Snowball followed by several Port and Lemons, whereas when he had last seen her she was drinking pints of mild. He, meanwhile, being extremely conscious about not drinking and driving, but also extremely thirsty, drank several pints of lemonade while they talked and laughed about university (she hoped to go to East Anglia in October) and life in general. As the evening wore on, he began to feel her leg rubbing against his under the table and kept thinking about Geoff Boycott grinding out a four-hour hundred against the University at Fenners in order not to let his excitement show.

"Fancy coming to a party at Michelle's?" she asked as closing time approached. "Her parents are away and it should be good fun."

Nigel accepted with some enthusiasm and they drove to the party, which was very near to his parents' house. It turned out to be a typical teenage party with all of the males of the species shoe-horned into the kitchen to be near the collection of Watneys' Party Sevens (large tins which perversely contained just under six pints of bitter) while the girls danced alone in the living room.

Leaving Debbie to dance with some of her friends, he went to get her a drink and was pleasantly surprised to bump into a couple of old school friends, Graham Hughes (invariably known as Emlyn) and Nick Wooldridge.

"Doris! How's life in that last bastion of elitism?" asked Nick who had recently finished his second year at Essex University.

"Oh, pretty much the same as anywhere else, I guess" replied Nigel cheerfully. "The beer is cheap and in plentiful supply - pity I can't say the same about the girls, but c'est la vie."

"Whatever you do, Nigel, don't get Nick started on politics" counselled Graham. "Two years at Essex and our Nicholas is expressing political views that make Karl Marx sound like Genghis Khan."

This was Nick's cue to launch into a tirade against the policies of Prime Minister Jim Callaghan and his Chancellor, Denis Healey ("a footstool for the dark forces of capitalism") and about the need for a "proletarian dictatorship" – although, when pressed, he was apparently unable to be specific as to exactly what that would involve, except that Callaghan and Healey, along with Margaret Thatcher and Edward Heath, could expect to spend the rest of their lives in a British equivalent of Siberia.

The argument continued for some time until the sound of Chicago's *If You Leave Me Now* prompted Nigel to remember that he had still not given Debbie her drink and (more importantly) to realise that if he was going to make his move on her, this was his big opportunity.

"Excuse me, boys, I'd better go and find Debbie for a dance-can't leave the lady on her own for too long."

"You watch out there, mate" cautioned Graham, jokingly. "She's quite a girl is young Debbie-she'll eat you for breakfast."

Nigel waved his hand dismissively-no longer was he the callow youth who had bottled out when he had the chance to kiss Jane. He was now a conqueror and breaker of girls' hearts.

It was with a confident swagger that he strode through the living room door, where he promptly tripped over a couple of bodies and spilled the drinks. Turning to berate them for lying in such a stupid place, he saw a hairy creature (presumably male) with a female form wrapped round it that, on closer inspection, turned out to be Debbie. On seeing him she gave a small and slightly apologetic smile - speech would have been impossible with her tongue down the creature's throat and vice-versa - before turning her full attention back to the matter in hand.

He felt absolutely mortified: I cannot believe this. I am a Cambridge undergraduate and presumably not a complete air-head-in fact, I have every confidence that one day I will become a partner in a top law firm or a leading Q.C; I may not be a dead ringer for Robert Redford, but I am not exactly physically repulsive; she has obviously enjoyed my company and what really goes against the grain is that I have spent a small fortune (by my standards) on plying her with Snowballs and other foul concoctions, and yet, despite all of these things, I turn my back for just a few minutes (to get the little cow a drink) and next thing she is engaged in a pre-mating ritual with something that looks remarkably like the Missing Link. What did Virgil say? *Varium et mutabile mass femina*-a woman is a fickle and changeable creature. He was dead right there. Seething with rage, he left the party without saying goodbye to his friends or to the hostess and never saw Debbie again.

In the fullness of time, he was appalled at how he had been so outraged at what he saw as Debbie's treachery, when he had not hesitated to ride roughshod over Sally's feelings-and had done so with barely a second thought-at the prospect of a passionate fling with Debbie. At the time, however, he felt much less philosophical about the whole episode and with bad grace channelled his energies into a holiday job cleaning cars on the forecourt of a local dealer - before heading off on a month's Inter-Railing holiday in Europe with Pete and Roger (memorably, they left on the day that Elvis Presley died and returned to the news that T-Rex's Marc Bolan had been killed in a car crash earlier that day).

There was however one further frisson of romantic excitement, while he was still working at the garage, when he was asked one afternoon to deliver a new S-registration Ford Fiesta to a Mrs Robson who lived in Himley, a small village a few miles from Dudley.

"You can get the bus back from there - don't worry about coming back to work, though" he was told by the salesman. "Do you know Sue Robson? She's a bit of a looker - her husband is Derek Robson of Robson Steels. She used to drive a Jag. but the business isn't doing too well, by all accounts, and she's having to move down market."

It was a lovely July afternoon and Nigel was glad of the trip out into the country. Even the fact that, on the way, every radio station seemed to be playing *Ma Baker* by Boney M failed to lower his spirits. He found the house easily, pulled up on the drive and rang the bell. There was no reply so he walked round the side of the house and found Mrs Robson lying on a sun lounger in the garden wearing a bikini and holding a drink.

"I've come to deliver the new car," he mumbled. "I'm sorry - I did ring the bell but there was no reply."

"Don't worry. You'd have caught me wearing even less if you'd arrived a few minutes ago. Let's have a look at this car, then".

She put on a tee shirt and then they went round to the front of the house.

"Just look at it! What a tinny little thing! Derek thinks I need to drive round in a heap of trash like this to 'give the right signals' to the unions - thinks it will encourage them to accept a lower pay rise. Pillock! If he spent less time at the golf course and with his queer friends from his Masonic lodge the company wouldn't be in such a mess.

She smiled apologetically.

"What do they call you anyway?"

"I'm Nigel Troy."

"Come and have a drink, Nigel."

She led him into the house, put Donna Summer's *I Feel Love* on the record player and poured herself a gin and tonic from a cocktail cabinet, which played *My Way* when she opened the door. "What would you like?

"I'd love a beer please, Mrs Robson."

She laughed and looked at him teasingly. "Mrs Robson? How formal. You can call me Sue - or would you like me to be your Mrs Robinson? Long Life or Double Diamond?"

As she poured him a Double Diamond from a can, he glanced round the room and noted a photograph of a young-looking Sue in her wedding dress, smiling at a well-groomed but rather weak-looking older man, whom he assumed to be the infamous Derek. She could only have been about twenty, he decided, so it was probably taken about ten years previously.

He felt a surge of genuine sadness for her - he imagined her as having married a rich businessman (second or third generation wealth, he guessed) in the hope of finding happiness in material things, only to wind up a discontented wife, surrounded by the trappings of wealth but married to a man that she did not love.

I guess every form of refuge has its price, he thought to himself as she beckoned him to the imitation black leather sofa.

"So, Nigel, you are a student, are you?" she smiled. "Where at?"

""I'm reading law at Cambridge."

"Cambridge? Very impressive-how would you like to take me to one of your May Balls."

He flushed. "I'd love to - but I can't imagine that your husband would like it very much."

"Derek can naff off, as far as I'm concerned. Anyway, what are you doing spending your summer delivering cars? I'd have thought you'd be off gallivanting round the world."

"I'm going Inter-Railing round Europe in August, Sue, with some friends from Cambridge. I'm just doing this to earn the money."

"Can't be bad. Can I come and share your sleeping bag?"

When *I feel love* ended, she put on another Donna Summer record, *Love To Love You Baby,* and he did his best to carry on some sort of sensible discourse with Ms Summer's orgasmic moans in the background - to make matters worse, it was the fifteen minute album version and Sue began to mime the song during the (increasingly frequent) pauses in their conversations, making him more and more hot and flustered, to (he suspected) her immense enjoyment.

"Do you have a girlfriend in Cambridge?"

He stared fixedly at his beer, unable to return her gaze.

"No. Well...I did have, but we split up at the end of term."

"Shame. You make sure that you have your fun while you can. You know what they say-all work and no play.... Mind you, I'm a fine one to talk-a corpse would be more fun in bed than my dear husband.""Well goodbye, Nick" she said when he stood up to leave. "Enjoy the rest of your vacation. If you're ever at a loose end, you'd be very welcome to come and do the garden for me. I couldn't pay you anything, but you'd find me great entertainment."

Was she making fun of him? It was obvious that she enjoyed flirting with him and making him feel uncomfortable but was that as far as it went? Later he berated himself for not having the savoir-faire to handle the situation, but at the time he simply felt confused and relieved to be able to make a hasty retreat to the bus stop.

Some years later, he had been idly reading a newspaper story about a "black widow" who had "ensnared" a rich elderly man and then apparently murdered him, with the help of her "toy boy" lover, a nineteen year old media studies student from Sutton Coldfield: the story described how her first husband, a wealthy Midlands-based businessman, had died in mysterious circumstances and how, after the death of husband number two, his body had been exhumed and a post-mortem had revealed that he too had been murdered. To his amazement, he saw that the first husband was Derek Robson and realised that the lady concerned was the Sue Robson who had flirted with him all those years ago.

Had the unfortunate Derek signed his own death warrant when he made his wife drive a Ford Fiesta? he wondered. Did she ensnare her toy boy over a glass of beer from the cocktail cabinet and seduce him into committing murder most foul?

Despite the apparent brutality of the crime, he felt sad to think of the once-gorgeous Sue serving a life sentence in jail and forever afterwards would raise a glass of Double Diamond to her in his mind whenever he heard *Love To Love You Baby*.

At the time, though, the incident only served to make him regret having kicked Sally into touch (as Roger charmingly put it) and resolve to try to win her back when they returned to Cambridge. You don't know what you've got till its gone, he said to himself over and over again.

In the end, though, he simply did not have the courage to telephone her and resigned himself to having lost her forever. He did in fact see her at a Union Society disco a few weeks into the term – by then Punk had arrived and Norman Greenbaum and Steppenwolf had gone, to be replaced by *No More Heroes* and *Sheena is a Punk Rocker*. Sally was laughing and talking with a fresh-faced, wholesome looking lad while others pogoed around them and Nigel knew that it was too late, she had moved on. It was only then that it occurred to him for the first time that the reason why she showed so little emotion when he ended the relationship might have been that she was tiring of him and was relieved not to have to do the dirty work herself.

Despite that, he invited her to the 21st birthday party that he and Roger gave in the Summer Term but all that happened was that he received a pleasant but formal reply declining his invitation and he never saw her again.

Might she be contactable via the school reunion website? he wondered. But would it be wise to do so? Part of him hoped that she was happily married and leading a contented life, while a less honourable part liked to think that she might occasionally be longing to hear from him again.

The chances of her having signed up to the Friends Reunited site were, he knew, extremely remote but he still went over to the computer, logged on, found the site and entered the name of her school and then the year when she would have left (1978). To his delight (but also with some apprehension) he saw that her name was there.

Clicking on it, he found some very brief notes for her:

Sally Peters.

Happily unmarried, living and teaching in West London

Chapter 6

In some ways, he thought, it would have been easier if she had said that she had been married for 20 years, had 15 children and was blissfully happy or that she was living with a 28 year old toy boy-at least then he would have known that she was spoken for and that it was most unlikely that she ever gave him a moment's thought. Somehow it seemed more culpable-more disloyal to Amanda-to contact her when he knew that she was single and apparently unattached.

On the other hand, he was so curious to find out about her and (to be perfectly honest) whether she might think of him once in a while-or even harbour some residual feelings for him.

He typed a brief e-mail and then deleted it without sending it; he typed another one and then pressed "send" quickly, before he could change his mind.

To: Sally Peters
From: Nigel Troy
Presumably you are the Sally Peters I used to know in Cambridge in the 1970s. If so, what are you up to and how is life treating you?
Best regards.
Nigel Troy.

The following evening, his heart leaped when he saw that she had replied:

To: Nigel Troy
From: Sally Peters
Nigel, what a surprise! Yes, one and the same! I am fine thank you, living in Ealing and teaching English at a local school - trying to eradicate rogue apostrophe's and the sort of tortured grammar we was never allowed to write!.
Those halcyon days in Cambridge seem a long time ago – whatever happened to you?
Sally.

To: **Sally Peters**
From: Nigel Troy
I am living in London too and lecturing in tax law – every bit as dull as it sounds.

I live in Islington and have been married to Amanda Cadogan, a hotshot corporate finance lawyer, for nearly 20 years. I am embarrassed to say that I am officially now Nigel Cadogan-Troy.

We have two children – Matt (18) and Galadriel (16).

I am told that I have not changed one jot since Cambridge – OK, the beard has gone (but quite recently) but I still listen to the Strawbs and Bob Dylan, rather than S-Club.

In fact, I think I still have my collection of flares somewhere....
Nigel

To: **Nigel Troy**
From: Sally Peters
Galadriel ??!!

Is Amanda a big Barclay James Harvest fan? (Remember going to see them at the Corn Exchange?).
Sally.

To: **Sally Peters**
From: Nigel Troy
She had the sheer bad luck to be born during Amanda's Middle Earth period – my fault for buying her the Lord of the Rings while she was pregnant. If it had been a boy she wanted to call him Aragon or Sauron – hormones all over the place and I was powerless to resist.

She likes to be known as Ria now – come to think of it, with her Gothic look, Gollum might have been an appropriate name.

Anyhow, what have you been up to over the last 25 years?
Nigel.

To: **Nigel Troy**
From: Sally Peters
I went to Nottingham Uni to read English, trained as a teacher then went off to India to work in a home for the mentally handicapped – originally

63

only for 12 months but I wound up staying 9 years!

When I came back, I got a job teaching English at a school in West London and have stayed there ever since. I live in a flat in Ealing.

As you will have seen, I have never married - I guess I never met the right person (yet!) Maybe I missed out on all that by spending my prime years in India.

I wouldn't have missed that time for the world, though – a great experience and so worthwhile. Have you ever been there?

And tell me about Amanda!

Sally

To: Sally Peters
From: Nigel Troy

Roger and I spent a month or so backpacking around India and Nepal when we had finished our Law Society Finals and before starting work. We did the usual tourist bit – travelled overland from Delhi to Kathmandu, saw the Taj Mahal etc. Then we flew down to Calcutta and back from there.

I loved it – so much to see, the noise, the smells (especially the smells) – but must admit that sometimes I wondered if I should just have had a few curries on Brick Lane, gone on to a sun bed and taken plenty of laxatives.

Calcutta was an amazing city – we had an eventful stay there.

Anyhow, Amanda: we met when we worked at the same law firm in the early 1980s – Our Tune was Seven Tears by the Goombay Dance Band. She went onto great things – I didn't. I guess I just didn't fit into the mould (they don't like beards at law firms - Beard Envy I call it) and I wound up an academic (Hackney is a far cry from Cambridge, though!).

She is blonde (not entirely natural…), attractive and one of the City's leading deal doers.

She talks almost entirely in impenetrable jargon-market caps, internal rates of return, leverage, due diligence, deal-breakers-and is always working on an all-consuming deal – each one with a code name, normally extremely dull and unimaginative. The only one I liked was when they were buying a spring manufacturing company and called it Project Zebedee- -and there was a deal involving a business on Tyneside which became Project Gazza, come to think of it.

Apart from work and her bi-weekly sessions in the gym with her personal fitness trainer (a sickeningly sun-bronzed South African called Russell) her only other passion is colonic irrigation - she is almost evangelical about it.

But back to 1977: can you remember the first record that we danced to?

Nigel.

To: Nigel Troy
From: Sally Peters
Pass! Farmer Bill's Cowman by the Wurzels?
Sally.

To: Sally Peters
From: Nigel Troy
Wrong: it was Young Hearts Run Free by Candi Staton.
Nigel.

To: Nigel Troy
From: Sally Peters
Wow! I am impressed! I never had you down as the sentimental type – your idea of a romantic night out was a trip to the Panton Arms with Pete and Roger, I seem to recall. Appropriate title though - I seem to remember you deciding on Jubilee Day that it was time for your young heart to run free............

Anyhow, what was that album you used to play all the time? There was a track about angels that I really liked.

And how are Pete and Roger? Do you keep in touch?
Sally.

To: Sally Peters
From: Nigel Troy
Pete and Roger are living and working in or around London so I see them fairly often. They are in good form.

Pete has been married for 20 years or so to Sue and they have three children (I am godfather to the oldest, James).

Roger is about to tie the knot for the third time to a lovely doctor called Jackie, having apparently lost his penchant for nymphettes at long last. I hope this will be "it" now-he has cost me a fortune in wedding presents and stag weekends! The last stag weekend lasted almost as long as the marriage.

Pete rather offended him by asking if it was possible to buy a season ticket for his weddings.

Anyhow, the song: "Oh lord give us a sign that soon we may taste angel wine"?

If that was the one you meant, the album was Strawbs' Ghosts – the track was called Angel Wine. That was my favourite too.

Ria's boyfriend, Kieran, has endeared himself to me by describing Strawbs as "wicked". There is hope for the younger generation yet....

Sally, why don't we meet up sometime for a drink or a bite to eat? It would be great to see you.

N.

To: Nigel Troy
From: Sally Peters
I would love to see you again, Nigel, but would it be a good idea? Too much water has passed under the bridge, I am afraid, so best not. Autre place, autre vie and all that.

Happy to keep in contact by e-mail though....
Sally.

Chapter 7

Feeling decidedly flat after the exchange of e-mails with Sally (which had initially seemed to hold such promise) had ended, with what appeared to him to be a very firm brush-off, for a few days he could not summon the enthusiasm even to open his mailbox to check his e-mails but when he finally got round to it, he was amazed as ever by the veritable smorgasbord of subjects covered by the array of unsolicited messages that confronted him-who ever could have imagined that civilisation could have descended to this?

Last time I had so much spam was in the days of school dinners, he said to himself, remembering the days when he would be forced by the dinner ladies to sit at the table until he had eaten it all. On one occasion he had still been there at going home time, eating tiny morsel after tiny morsel, all the while trying not to retch.

Another of the (limited number of) benefits of being 46, he decided, was that never again would he be forced to eat spam or corned beef-or, at least, not until he was in his twilight years and completely lost his marbles and all other faculties. by when he would probably be beyond caring.

As it was, one of his (in his opinion, decidedly few) remaining avenues of pleasure was to send what he considered to be suitably witty replies to these junk e-mails and that was how he began to amuse himself that evening:

To: *Nigel Troy*
Subject: *Viagra by male (!) order - Wow!*
As a gentleman of a certain age, do you sometimes feel in need of a little something to "boost your confidence"? Take advantage of our special offer of a month's supply of Viagra tablets for only £2.50 (plus p&p). Neither you (nor your loved ones!) will be disappointed.
To order, click here without delay.
To be taken off the circulation list, go to

www.wow!factor//179643//GAB//489LZ.co.uk

Outraged at the suggestion that he, Nigel Troy, might be impotent at the age of 46 he replied.
Yo, man, you trying to send coals to Newcastle?
N. Troy.

To: ***Nigel Troy***
Subject: ***Cash deposit***
Greetings, Mr Troy.
Allow me to introduce myself: from 1989 to 1998 I was Finance Minister of a West African republic, during which time I deposited sums totalling US$8.5 million in a personal bank account in Zurich.

I am writing to you as an individual of reputation and discretion in order to request your assistance in helping me to access these funds.

In return for your assistance you will receive US$6.5 million and will pay me just US$2 million.

All you have to do is to e-mail to me by return your bank account details and your passport number, together with its date and place of issue. The money will then be transferred to your account within one week.

I await your immediate response.
Your obedient servant
Cornelius P. Dicker

A mischievous idea occurred to him and he replied:

My dear Mr. Dicker
You are labouring under a serious misapprehension as I am the Chief Rodent Officer for the Isle of Dogs and unable to assist with your venture.

However, my esteemed friend, James Granville at Bodkin Manners, solicitors of London, will be pleased to help.

Please contact him at your earliest convenience on james.Granville@bodkinmanners.com.
Yours truly
Nigel Troy Dip. Stick.

To: *Nigel Troy*
Subject: *Breast enlargement*
Dissatisfied with your figure? Want to maximise your assets? Then click here to take advantage of our breast enlargement programme as followed by Page 3 Girls and Supermodels Galore!

Do these spam merchants not even check the sex of their victims? he wondered.
Thank you very much for your concern but I will let nature take its course first of all and will make a note to contact you if dissatisfied with my figure when I am 18.
Yours
Nigella Troy (aged 6)

To: *Nigel Troy*
Subject: *Thai Women looking for British Men*
Still looking for that special someone? Then look no further!
Visit us here and find the woman of your dreams.
You can browse through our pictures and bios of beautiful Thai women looking for a Western man like you.
Click here for the start of a relationship that may last a lifetime.
Twenty years too late, he thought to himself, sadly, but replied:
Thank you-could be interested, but would you be prepared to take a 44-year old corporate finance lawyer (with attitude) in part exchange?

To: *Nigel Troy*
Subject: *HRT*
As a lady of a certain age, do you long to sample the elixir of perpetual youth and recapture the magic of your younger days? Then click here to take advantage of our special hormone replacement treatment programme now!
Thousands of women will confirm how their lives have been rejuvenated in this way, but just listen to Mrs Edna Grubb of Newport Pagnell:
"At 53 I could feel my vitality ebbing away but after 3 months' HRT treatment I have the libido of a 20-year old and a body to match."

He replied:

Sirs, from my name you may have divined that I was of the male, er, gender but perhaps you may still be able to help me.

My hairline is receding and most of my faculties are gradually failing but meanwhile I still have to shave every day and indeed hairs are beginning to grow out of my nostrils, my ears and every other orifice you might care to name (and indeed some which you might not care to name).

Would HRT help to alleviate the problem?

Alternatively, could you let me have Mrs. Grubb's phone number?

To: Nigel Troy
Subject: Your favourite Soap Stars Naked, Nigel
Nigel, fancy seeing your favourite soap stars in the nude? Then click here without delay.

To unsubscribe, go to www.naked_TV-stars.145//:6767/?//gsb478. co.uk

He replied:

Thank you-unfortunately I am unable to find any nude pictures of Ena Sharples on your nice little site. Are you able to oblige?

He was about to log off when a new e-mail flashed up on his screen:

To: Nigel Troy
From: Sally Peters
How silly of me! It would be fun to meet you again after all these years - to see what the ravages of time have done to you, if nothing else....
Next week is half term - would you be free any time?
Sally

To: Sally Peters
From: Nigel Troy
I have a clear day next Tuesday - how about meeting up then? What time would suit you? I am free all day.
Nigel

To: *Nigel Troy*
From: *Sally Peters*
Mid-day? Where?
Sally

To: **Sally Peters**
From: *Nigel Troy*
Regents Park - Clarendon Gate?
Nigel

To: *Nigel Troy*
From: **Sally Peters**
See you there....

Chapter 8

As the day of their meeting approached, Nigel felt a mounting sense of excitement at the prospect of seeing Sally again. The omens, he felt, were particularly promising as, on the Bank Holiday Monday, Wolverhampton Wanderers had beaten Sheffield United three-nil in the first division play-off final to regain their place in the top flight of English football after a nineteen year absence-and he was certain that three-nil was the score by which they had beaten Liverpool on that far-off weekend when he and Sally had first met.

Amanda was working and Matt had gone on a cultural weekend visit to Dublin with his rugby club friends, while Galadriel was still in bed when he left the house and unlikely to surface for the foreseeable future, so there was nobody who needed an explanation of where he was going-or, he thought wistfully, who was likely to be remotely interested.

Sally was already at the Clarendon Gate when Nigel arrived. It was a warm day and she was wearing light grey trousers and a plain, white T-shirt and Nigel was surprised how little she had changed - there was no hint of grey in her hair (which was shoulder length) and her face was unlined, save for some laughter lines around her eyes.

She kissed him quickly on the cheek and then they went for a slow walk around the park. He tried to make conversation but, to his disappointment, she was very monosyllabic and kept her eyes firmly on the ground.

Eventually she blurted out: "Come on then, Nigel, what made you get in touch with me after all these years? Is it a mid-life crisis or doesn't your wife understand you?"

"It's more that I don't understand her!" was his reply, then: "Neither, really, Sally, I guess I have often wondered what happened to you and wanted to find out. No ulterior motives."

"I'm sorry, Nigel. I was really looking forward to seeing you but now I feel guilty even though I do know that we aren't really doing anything wrong. That's just me, I'm afraid."

He was unable to think of anything constructive to say, so they carried on walking in near silence, until he suggested an early lunch in a café on the park, which she accepted with evident relief.

Sally chose a salad, Nigel a lasagne and when they sat down at a table in the sun he raised his glass to her and said in his best Humphrey Bogart voice: "Here's looking at you, kid." She laughed and asked:
"Do you remember when we went to see that film?"
"Of course - a Friday night at the Arts Cinema. Pete and Roger came too, I think."
"Of course."
"When we came out it was snowing and I walked you home."
"Ever the gentleman, weren't you? Didn't we wind up building a snowman on Jesus Green?"
"That's right - there was some sort of end-of-term disco going on at Jesus College and we could hear the music really clearly across the green, so we danced in the snow."
"I suppose you are going to tell me that you remember what it was we danced to."
"Even I'm not quite that sad - that time probably was the Wurzels."
"I do remember that we had a lengthy debate about whether Rick did the right think in putting the Ingrid Bergman character (Ilsa, was it?) on the plane with her husband or whether he should have gone with her and abandoned Laszlo to his fate. Like the good convent-educated girl I was - and still am - I thought he did right but I seem to recall that you, Mr Romantic, didn't see why her being married and the fight against totalitarianism should stand in the way of true love."
"That sounds about right - I can't say that I've thought much about this particular dilemma over the last 25 years or so but I guess I still think he should have got on the plane."
"Perhaps someone will do a re-make set in the 1970s Cambridge. Rick and Laszlo could wear enormous flares and Sam could play - what do you think?"
"Something deep and meaningful like *Sugar Baby Love* or *I'd Like To Teach The World To sing*? They don't write them like that any more."
"There's something to be thankful for."
"I bet Cambridge is just beginning to become over-run with tourists-do you get back there much?"
"Pretty regularly. My parents still live in the same house and it's always

a good antidote to London, although it's changed a lot in recent years-a fair bit more gentrified for a start."

" I can remember that house really well - and that dog that you used to have-a real Heinz Fifty Seven Varieties- with a very literary name. Bingley was it?"

"You must be thinking of Heathcliff-we used to love wandering over Jesus Green on wild winter nights calling 'Heathcliff, Heathcliff.' It could hardly have been further removed from Wuthering Heights country, but it kept us amused."

"It seemed very sophisticated to me-we must have been the only family in the world who actually called their dog Rover."

"We moved with the times in the end-after Heathcliff died, we had two cats called Duran and Duran. Duran got run over by a milk float at a tragically young age but Duran kept going until a few years ago."

"I wish I could credit my family with such cultural awareness-Rover was followed by either Fido or Bonzo. I can't remember which way round it was now."

" Do you visit Dudley very often or are you too much of a metropolitan sophisticate for that now?"

"I haven't been back to Dudley for years. My parents moved out to Shropshire towards the end of my time at Cambridge."

"That sounds nice-did they retire there?"

"Far from it. It was really weird actually: my father was your typical *Semi-Detached Suburban Mr. James*-worked in middle management, cleaned the car every Sunday afternoon, his idea of excitement was mowing the lawn - you know the type - then out of the blue I had a letter from him to say that he had had enough of the closed shop, demarcation disputes and all the industrial problems that seemed to be everywhere in those days and that they were going to do a Good Life. They had found a small house near Bridgnorth with a decent plot of land and they had decided to trade in the budgie for some Rhode Island Reds, buy a goat and a few sheep and get back to the land and set their souls free.

"I tried to explain that the Good Life was only a television comedy series and that Richard Briars and Felicity Kendal didn't really opt for an alternative lifestyle in Surbiton, but he wasn't having any of it. I think he thought we could all live out there in this rural idyll like the Waltons or Little House On The Prairie.

"I'm just thankful that it was the Good Life that was his favourite programme rather than Reginald Perrin-otherwise I might have received a telegram to say that his clothes had been found on the canal tow-path and that he was missing, presumed dead.

"Amanda of course claims that this all goes to show that under-achievement is in my genes but in fact my father went on to do extremely well for himself-he began supplying produce to local shops in the days before anybody knew what 'organic' meant and then suddenly there was a real demand for it and he built up a successful business. He's retired now, but still living out in the Boondocks. Probably growing his own dope, for all I know. It's lovely where they are, actually, in the Severn Valley. The only drawback is that they have severe flood warnings for the rest of the year but a hosepipe pan every July and August-this is Britain, after all."

Sally laughed: "good for your parents. Shame you didn't go back there and become Shropshire's answer to John-Boy-but perhaps Amanda will go through a Damascene conversion one day and the two of you can grow organic cauliflowers in your garden in Islington. Or would she be a Margot rather than a Barbara?"

" I'm not sure she's either really-I can't see her spending her days flower arranging or going to Pony Club meetings, with a *Young Farmers Do It In Wellies* sticker on her Porsche. Amanda's idea of down-shifting would be to leave the office in daylight hours once in a while-that's why I was the one who wound up in academia."

"So what are your students like?"

" There are a couple who show the odd spark of intelligence but the others appear to have been lobotomised at birth and, I suspect, want to be there even less than I do.

"There's one clique of peroxide blondes with rings or studs in every visible part of their anatomies who always spend the whole class discussing the events of the previous evening and planning their social lives for the night ahead; there's a group of blokeish individuals with knuckles trailing along the floor, who always arrive half way through the lecture nursing perpetual hangovers-and then the rest, whose idea of entertainment seems to be to start a Mexican Wave whenever they find the subject a bit dull. Which, when you are lecturing on tax, means that the lecture room is one never-ending Mexican Wave."

"At my school the boys just spend their time eyeing up the totty while the girls spend theirs texting each other surreptitiously whenever they think Im not looking. It seems poles apart from my time at the Convent- I dread to think what the nuns would have made of modern teenage life. I remember a Sister Esmeralda who thought that Alice Cooper was demonically possessed."

" All very different from your time in Calcutta - did you find it a real cultural shock?"

"Just a bit. I'll never forget my first day there: I went for a walk on Chowringhee and in seconds I had attracted this crowd of children all calling out 'one Rupee, one pen.' It was crazy. In the end, I escaped to the Maidan, which was a real oasis of peace and tranquillity. I got used to the hustle and bustle in time, though. Britain seems very laid back by comparison."

He laughed: " I have fond memories of spending a Sunday afternoon on the Maidan; there were lots of games of cricket going on and because I was an Englishman with a beard they got it into their heads that I was Ian Botham and kept getting me to bowl at them. I know what you mean about the sheer number of people, though: I remember feeling completely overwhelmed when I arrived in Delhi-particularly when we walked along Chandni Chowk on the first morning. Then we went to the Red Fort and came across a couple of middle-aged Brits. who had just been mugged by a bunch of schoolgirls."

" How come?"

"The way they described it was that they'd just got into an auto rickshaw when they were surrounded by these girls: there was a swirl of saris, then some of the girls were poking their fingers into their eyes and while they put their hands up to protect their faces the other girls went through their pockets and their bags. Idiots, they had their passports and all their money on them, so they couldn't even pay the rickshaw driver his five Rupee fare."

"That's a good story but if I'd have been them I would have invented a rather more heroic tale to explain why I had lost my money-at the very least it would have been a posse of armed dacoits rather than a bunch of delinquent ten-year olds."

" Do you remember those characters in Delhi who used to wander round the centre of Connaught Place with little packets of cotton wool buds?"

" Yes, I do. Very persistent they were too-there was one bloke who must have sat on the grass next to me for a good hour, with his tattered little notebook of testimonies from suckers of different nationalities whom he'd done over the years, all saying how great their hearing was afterwards but no doubt they're all learning to lip-read by now.

The technique I worked out for dealing with them and with anybody else who hassled me and wouldn't take 'no' for an answer was to pretend not to understand English and then jabber back to them in my best schoolgirl Latin. Just repeating 'veni, vidi, vici' and 'amo, mass, amat' normally did the trick, but as a last resort I used to give them an ablative absolute-that never failed."

"Good one, Sally: I must try that with these people who come on the phone trying to persuade me to buy double glazing or to re-mortgage the house-a quick blast of Homer's Iliad should do nicely. Do I even need to ask whether you visited the Taj Mahal?"

"Of course - I managed to tick off pretty well all of the Lonely Planet Guide's 'Must Sees' while I was there. I'd seen it so many times in pictures that I expected to be a bit disappointed by it - sometimes places like that turn out to be a bit disappointing in real life, don't they? That certainly wasn't the case with the Taj though - I went back several times over the years and it seemed to get more and more impressive somehow."

"I thought it was brilliant too but I must admit that the day I spent there was one of the grimmest I have ever known."

"How come?"

"I think I must have had a dodgy meal the night before or maybe some mineral water that was straight from the tap-whatever it was, I woke up in the early hours feeling like death warmed up-the Oboe Syndrome!"

"What do you mean?"

"Open at Both Ends."

"Thank you for sharing that with me, Nigel!   I do sympathise though."

"Yeah, I don't think I've ever felt worse.

"Anyhow, I finally dragged myself out of bed around lunchtime and took a rickshaw to the Taj. My abiding memory is of going inside and the noise and the smells-a delicate blend of incense, sweat and urine odours –made me feel decidedly unwell again. In the end, I had to rush out and adjourn to the Taj Café for some hot, black tea. I'd love to go back there one day and really do it justice."

Sally laughed: "tell me about your adventures in Calcutta."

"We stayed at the Fairlawn Hotel-did you ever go there? It was still run by an elderly British couple who had 'stayed on' after independence and it was wonderful. A bit more expensive than our normal accommodation but it was worth it: the rooms were good, the food was excellent and they even served blancmange for tea.

"We went on an organized bus tour of the city but we spent most of it stuck in traffic jams on that busy road that leads up to Delhi eventually-what's it called?"

"The Grand Trunk Road?"

"Yeah, that's it. Anyway, we got fed up with the bus and so when we got to the Howrah Bridge we got off and went to have a look at the river.

"There was a great photo of the bridge in our Lonely Planet Guide and so I asked Roger to take my photo in front of it, then we walked further along the river and photographed it some more.

"Suddenly, three unprepossessing characters appeared from nowhere and grabbed hold of us and then told us that they were plain clothes police and that they were arresting us for being Pakistani spies."

"An obvious conclusion to jump to, I'm sure" she laughed.

"Quite: we assumed that they just wanted some *baksheesh* to make them go away and so Roger waved a few Rupees at them but they just called us every name under the sun and then bundled us into a car and took as to a police station.

"It was quite comical: there was a rather bored-looking sergeant on duty who was idly putting rubber stamps on pieces of paper and who barely looked up when we came in, until our captors shouted out that they had caught some spies photographing the bridge—which was the cue for frenetic activity, or what passes for frenetic activity on the sub-continent. Armed police seemed to be appearing all over the place.

"I think that even then we might have got away with paying the officers on duty a few hundred Rupees to let us go, but Roger began to revel on his role and kept bowing and saying '007 at your service' and 'my name is Bond, Premium Bond.'"

"Hmm, I bet that went down well-Indian officialdom is not exactly renowned for its humour."

"So we discovered: the comedy sure came to an end when they threatened to break his legs and took us at gun-point to (separate) cells for interrogation. In the end, they told us that we were being charged with espionage and would appear before a magistrate the next morning.

"We spent the night in a tiny cell with some stale chapattis to eat and only cockroaches for company, then we came into court early the following morning.

"Luckily, the magistrate was a young woman – only about thirty, I would guess - and she told us that were charged with various offences under different sub-sections of some anti-espionage law and that we could plead guilty to a lesser charge and accept a fine of 1,500 Rupees each or wait to appear before a judge on something more serious, in which case he could give us up to 10 years."

"Not a difficult choice, I suspect?"

"Not in the slightest: we paid the fine with something approaching good grace – I can tell you that that night in the cell was the longest night of my life.

"Roger seemed totally unfazed by the whole thing – I think he rather fancied her and when he pleaded guilty and she told us she was fining us he winked at her and said 'thank you, Moneypenny.' Mercifully, I think his attempt at humour was lost on her."

"You were very lucky, Nigel" laughed Sally. "I can't imagine that life in prison in Calcutta bears much resemblance to Porridge - and the food would probably have made the Berni Inn in Cambridge seem like the Ritz by comparison. Did you never see Midnight Express?"

"I was certainly mighty relieved to get back to tea and blancmange at the Fairlawn-while Roger took great pleasure in regaling everyone there with the story, which of course he well and truly embellished, so that our fellow residents will still believe that it was only my lawyerly eloquence and Roger's boyish charm that saved us from being shot as spies."

"Did you manage to keep out of trouble after that?"

"Absolutely: we spent the rest of our time in Calcutta just strolling on the Maidan and searching for the Black Hole and then it was time to fly home. By then I was desperate to get out of India, but a few weeks later I was desperate to go back there-it's that sort of place, isn't it?"

"I was re-reading Midnight's children again a few weeks ago and that brought back a few memories: I read it the first time on a steam boat journey in Bangladesh, from Dhaka to a place called Khulna, and it will always remind me of that trip, which was wonderful. It sounds silly but I've never been anywhere that seemed quite so far from home and... well, foreign. I think it was because, in India, all the signs are in English and most people speak some English, but in Bangladesh everything was in Bengali and it was much harder to find my way around. I loved the country though-and the people are really friendly."

"Do you read a lot of books by Indian writers?"

"Quite a lot: in fact, Nigel, I did think of you a couple of years ago when I was reading a book called Inheritance by someone called Indira Ganesh. Have you read it?"

"I've never even heard of it."

"Well you should-just for one character, a holy man who comes out with these pearls of wisdom which, when you first read them, seem really profound but in fact are just snatches of Bob Dylan songs. It's really well done and it reminded me of you because you were always a big Dylan fan and because of your propensity to speak in song lyrics all the time."

"Song lyrics? What makes you say that?"

"In your conversations you always quoted from songs-quite subconsciously, I'm sure."

"It certainly was-nobody has ever told me that before. I don't know whether to believe you: can you give me any examples?"

"None specific after twenty five years or so but suppose the weather was dull: you might say that you hate days when the sun doesn't shine and it's cloudy and grey, oblivious (I assume) to the fact that you were actually quoting from *Remember You're A Womble*."

"I can't believe that I ever quoted from the Wombles, consciously or otherwise."

"I'm sure you would never have been so un-cool but you certainly used to come out with lines from songs that were a little less *infra dig*. I'm sure that when we met, your first chat-up line came from some song or other."

"I'm going to become really self-conscious about it now. You've given me an idea, though: I think I'll found a phoney religious cult and set myself up as its leader. I'll have all my followers sitting at my feet and hanging on my every word and I'll keep on coming out with quotes from Dylan or Strawbs like 'money doesn't talk, it swears' or 'the road to nowhere never climbs' and they'll all gasp in amazement at my wit and wisdom."

The conversations carried on in a pleasant and relaxed vein and Nigel felt sad when she announced that she had to go back to do some work.

"I've had a great time - I'd love to see you again" he ventured tentatively.

"I've had a lovely afternoon too - keep the e-mails coming" was her reply then she gave him a quick kiss on the cheek and disappeared into the bowels of the London Underground.

Chapter 9

Nigel arrived home in a very relaxed mood and whistling *I Lost My Heart To A Starship Trooper* for no particular reason.

"Hi, Dad" came the greeting from his daughter, who was in front of the mirror putting the finishing touches to her make-up (which he always assumed she must buy in bulk from some sort of cash-and-carry for funeral parlour operators). "How come you sound so, like, cheerful tonight?"

Nigel could feel himself begin to flush: "Oh, you know, guess the Prozac must be beginning to work - or maybe I overdosed on the St. John's Wort. Anyhow, where are you off to?"

"Kieran's band are, like, playing a gig at the Slug & Lettuce."

With that make-up and those clothes, I thought you were off Trick-Or-Treating, he thought to himself but thankfully refrained from saying out loud. "Any word from your mother?"

"Usual: she's stuck in a long, like, negotiating meeting on this big deal of hers - Project Britney. Anyway, she said not to wait up. See you later, Dad."

"Bye, darling, have a good time" he answered rather absent-mindedly as she went out through the door. Truth to tell, for once, he was not at all dismayed at the prospect of yet another evening home alone.

Feeling in the mood for something a little slushy, he put on Van Morrison's *Tupelo Honey* and then began to reflect on his day with Sally.

No question about it, she had been ill at ease to start with but had gradually relaxed and he was sure that she had had as good a time as he had. It was such a long time since he had enjoyed anybody's company so much - she was interesting to talk to and there had been plenty of laughs.

Taking a piece of paper, he began to write a brief comparison of the respective merits and de-merits of Sally and Amanda, in the hope that this might explain why he had been so captivated by Sally and why he felt such a distance between himself and Amanda.

Sally	*Amanda*
Pretty in an under-stated sort of way	*Extremely attractive-especially with make-up*
Delightful and surprisingly subversive sense of humour	*Mainly sarcasm*
Gentle and mild-mannered	*In your face*
Spiritual-quiet but strong faith	*A devoted servant of Mammon*
Laughs at my attempts at humour	*Doesn't listen to a word I say*
Seems interested in what I think and how I feel	*Too busy to care*
Our conversations are good	*What conversations?*
Could she have been my soul mate?	*Prefers working to mating*

There was the nub of it, he decided. Sally had shown him plenty of attention and made him feel that she was listening to what he had to say, while Amanda only ever seemed to have time for IPOs and leveraged buy-outs (whatever they were).

It had not always been like that, though, he thought as he remembered how he and Amanda had originally met when she came to work at Bodkin Manners as a trainee solicitor (or articled clerk, as they were still called in those days).

With her good looks and smart clothes, Amanda had soon caught his eye and he remembered her name appearing on the 1981 version of his list of The World's Most Beautiful Women, along with Debbie Harry,

Victoria Principal from Dallas and Siouxsie Sioux. Her cool demeanour in the office had, however, already earned her the sobriquet of the Ice Maiden and he had not even attempted to make conversation with her.

At the Bodkin Manners' Christmas party (held at a top London hotel) she wore a taffeta ball gown and looked absolutely stunning - a real eye-full as he commented to Mike Castaldo after dinner.

"Couldn't agree more, Nige - pity she's already spoken for, isn't it?"

"How do you know that?"

"She was with him at Geraldine's party - you were away that weekend, weren't you? He looked a complete dork, actually."

Mike's girlfriend, Sue, who was herself an articled clerk with the firm, came over to join them.

"Eyeing up the talent as ever, guys?"

"Perish the thought, Sue" laughed Nigel. "You know that Michael here only has eyes for you. I was just noting, from a purely aesthetic point of view, of course, how smart the lady over there looks tonight - you know, the one in the taffeta dress."

"The Ice Maiden? Got it from an Oxfam shop for a fiver, she claims".

"Mike tells me she's already attached - what a waste."

"She's got some guy in tow, but from what I hear it's rather a stormy relationship, although he is reputed to have one particularly attractive feature, which is the size of his bank balance."

"You don't think she would be attracted by a bijoux residence in Catford, then?"

"The omens don't look good, I'm forced to admit."

"What about that new girl in the Accounts department, Nige? The one with the face of an angel and (so I'm told) the morals of an alley cat."

"She only looks about twelve," laughed Sue. "I'm sure she'd regard Nigel as a fatherly figure rather than a likely candidate for a red hot lover."

"That's the story of my life-always too young, too old or too impoverished. All through my time at Cambridge I struggled to pull because I was too young; then, a few weeks ago, we went back and crashed a college disco, I asked a girl to dance and when I told her I was 24 she replied 'blimey, you're a bit old aren't you?' You obviously think it would be the same with Little Miss Double Entry over there. Was there ever a split second, a scintilla in time, when I was the right age to get off with somebody?"

"I'll have to pass on that one, but I don't think age will be your problem with the Ice Maiden - a well-proportioned wallet is what is called for. Didn't know the jacket pocket was such an erogenous zone, did you?"

"Looks like you've got to fall back on your natural wit and charm, then" added Mike. "So best forget it, eh?"

"Faint heart never won fair maiden though... or maybe she likes a bit of rough..."

"Thanks a bunch, Sue - you sure know how to massage my ego. She's meant to be moving to the Tax Department in January so I guess I'll just have to wow her with my encyclopaedic knowledge of Capital Transfer Tax rate bands... or lower my sights more than a little."

Amanda did move into his department after Christmas and he was delighted when he soon found himself working on a big deal with her, which involved several late evenings' work. Their conversations were always brisk and business-like but one evening he plucked up the courage to suggest that they adjourn for a drink.

"What an excellent idea" she smiled. "I think I've over-dosed on tax disclosures tonight."

They went to a nearby wine bar where he began his campaign to win her favour - mindful all the time of the nameless boyfriend who was presumably still waiting somewhere in the wings.

"So, Amanda, how are your articles going?" he asked, with as breezy an air as he could muster.

"Okay, I suppose - I like the firm but it would be nice to be given a bit more responsibility and to be allowed to do a bit more on my own."

He grinned. "Believe me, if they like you, they'll soon have you working all hours that God sends - and quite a few for which He is not responsible."

"That's fine by me - I'm not afraid of hard work."

Sensing that he was going to struggle to make much headway on work-related topics, he tried a more personal tack.

"Are you from London?"

"Well, from Surrey - Dorking actually."

"The Stockholder Belt, eh? Is your father Something In The City?"

"No, he's something in Guildford. An insurance broker to be more precise."

This is like drawing teeth, he groaned inwardly, before she carried on. "I'd guess that you're from up north somewhere."

"Not really... Worcestershire, actually."

"Worcestershire?" For the first time she became vaguely animated. "Isn't that near Birmingham?"

"Well... quite near, I suppose. Why do you ask?"

"The New Romantics scene there is supposed to be great. Do you ever go to the Rum Runner?"

"I don't think so; what is it, actually?"

"It's a club in Birmingham - where Duran Duran started out."

"Duran Duran?"

"Yes, you know, Simon Le Bon. They're brilliant, aren't they?"

"Oh, yeah, great - one of my favourites" he replied and wondered what they would sound like. "Is that the sort of stuff you're into?"

"Sure. Duran Duran are the best but I love Depeche Mode too.... And the Human League."

Nigel nodded, relieved to hear a name he recognised. "The Human League – they're the ones who did *Don't You Want Me Baby*, weren't they? Wasn't that the Christmas number one?"

"That's right - *Dare* is a great album."

"Oh, yeah, absolutely... one of my all-time favourites" he lied gamely. "They're a great band - and the one with the German name - Rudolf Hesse was it?"

She threw back her head and laughed. "I assume you mean Spandau Ballet!"

"Yes, of course. The lead guitarist's brilliant.... I think I prefer the Human League though.

"I quite like Led Zeppelin and Bob Dylan as well" he added, as if by way of an after-thought. "And I still listen to stuff like the Undertones and the Jam and that band who sang the song about the old lady in her candle-lit hovel. Squeeze was it?"

Sensing that she was unlikely to be impressed by his tastes in music, he decided to try another conversational gambit.

"What else do you do, when you're not being a lawyer?" he ventured.

"I like the theatre and the cinema. I'm a real Woody Allen nut-actually, don't take this the wrong way, Nigel, but there's something about you that reminds me of him.... And I used to play a lot of squash but don't seem to have had chance to find anywhere to play."

Carpe diem, he thought-seize the opportunity. "I'm a member of a club not far from the office-I'll give you a game some time, if you like."

"That would be lovely, thanks. When?"

"How about next week? We should have completed the American deal by then."

"Thursday?"

"That would be fine by me."

"Okay: just book a court and tell me when and where."

They had a competitive but enjoyable game of squash, which had the added bonus of allowing him to admire her long legs ("they go all the way up" was how he described them to Roger) and for a few weeks after that played once a week and always went for a leisurely drink afterwards, until he plucked up the courage to suggest going out for a meal instead-an invitation which she accepted with no obvious sign of reluctance.

In the restaurant, he attempted to wow her with his newfound knowledge of New Romantic music (acquired via Roger's younger sister) and began to enthuse over Visage, having recently bought a copy of *Fades To Grey* from a second hand shop.

"They're definitely the best band around at the moment" he pronounced with some satisfaction.

"What about Haircut 100?"

"Oh, yeah, they're pretty good, too."

"Even better than Adam Ant?"

"Hard to say" he frowned, before Amanda suddenly began to roar with laughter.

"You're so sweet, Nigel-pretending to like all this New Romantic stuff, when you're so obviously an unreconstructed 'seventies rocker."

"Am I really that transparent?" he asked sheepishly.

"Of course you are-you do make me laugh. You're really nice to me as well-that makes a change, I can assure you."

"What makes you say that?"

"Oh, nothing, really. It's just…no, forget it. I'm having a really nice time, let's not spoil it."

He was sure that she had come close to telling him about the well-heeled boyfriend who, he was now inclined to suspect, had either left the scene altogether or had suffered a serious fall from grace. He felt that for the first time he had penetrated behind the Ice Maiden mask-no mean feat in itself, he thought.

But she had no shortage of potential suitors within the firm- several of them much more senior than he was and with far more impressive bank balances. It seemed inconceivable that any feelings she had for him could be anything other than platonic.

A week or so later they were both invited to a party at the flat of one of the young lawyers in his department and Amanda turned up wearing a ra-ra skirt and a backless bat-wing top, while the other girls were nearly all wearing jeans and leg- warmers. From the moment she arrived, she was surrounded by what seemed to him to be a constant stream of eligible young males so he decided that there was no point in trying to compete with them for her affections and spent the evening talking to various friends, until at last she broke away and came over to where he was standing.

"Are you ignoring me tonight, Nigel?"

"Not deliberately, but you seem to have been surrounded by a cluster of admirers all evening-like bees round a honey pot."

"An occupational hazard" she laughed. "Are you going to dance with me?"

They began to dance to Soft Cell's *Tainted Love*, which, Nigel was delighted to find, turned out to be the long version, which led into *Where Did Our Love Go*.

The next record was a slow one and to his amazement she put her arms around his neck and held him close while they danced before letting him kiss her as the music ended.

Convinced that these signs of affection could only be attributed to a momentary lapse of reason and/or an excess of alcohol, it was with some diffidence that he asked her whether he could meet her for dinner one night the following week.

"I thought you'd never ask" she smiled. "Which night?"

"Monday?" he suggested, certain that if he left it any longer she would be bound to have met somebody else.

"That would be wonderful-I'll look forward to it" she replied, before putting her arms round his neck again and kissing him full on the lips.

After that they clearly regarded themselves as "an item" and were soon spending a lot of time together, with Nigel basking in the admiration of his peers as the man who had cracked the Ice Maiden.

Beneath the cool reserve, he found a lively sense of humour and a woman whose company he enjoyed immensely, while it was apparent that she liked his own sense of humour. Nevertheless, he never felt entirely sure of her affections and comments that she made from time to time made him feel sometimes that she was rather on the rebound from someone else-presumably the boyfriend Mike and Sue had mentioned at the office party.

She had a tendency suddenly to become very withdrawn and uncommunicative and on those occasions he would wait silently and nervously for her to tell him that it was all over between them, but somehow she always seemed to snap out of those reveries and everything would eventually revert to normal.

Matters continued in this way throughout that spring and early summer, until one night when he went round to her flat as arranged and, after he had rung her doorbell a few times, she came to the door looking very distraught.

"I'm sorry, Nigel, it's all so difficult, do you mind if we leave it until tomorrow?"

"What's the matter? Have you got somebody there?" She nodded wordlessly.

"Is it your ex?" The bloke you used to go out with?"

"Yes it is. I'm sorry, really sorry. I didn't invite him - he just turned up. I haven't seen him for months. I don't know what to do. Please give me some time - come round tomorrow night."

With a heavy heart, Nigel turned away with a muttered "goodnight, then." This, he feared, really was the end.

It was a lovely summer evening but a cloud of gloom had descended over him and he walked aimlessly round the neighbouring streets before taking a miserable Tube ride back to his own flat.

She was not in the office the following day and it was with a heavy heart that Nigel went round to her flat that evening. She offered him coffee and then they sat together in silence in front of Top of the Pops. Eventually Amanda broke the silence: "this is all so difficult and confusing. I should have been straighter with you."

He said nothing so she went on: "For most of my time at university I was going out with a bloke - it was all very intense and we lived pretty much in each others' pockets. It was all a lot of fun and I was besotted with him but about this time last year it all began to go horribly wrong - he became very moody and very possessive and I just couldn't stand it. Eventually, just after I started at Bodkin Manners, I ended the relationship and thought that he had accepted it.

"I hadn't heard from him again until last night when he turned up saying that he needed me and I think that that's probably right.

"I'm so sorry, Nigel, but I've thought about it a lot and I've got to see Tarquin again and give it another go."

"Tarquin!" exclaimed Nigel "what kind of a name is that?"

"Isn't his name a bit of a non-point, Nigel? The point is that I've decided to give him another chance - whatever his name is."

Nigel's misery on hearing these words was compounded by the fact that, at that very moment, Kid Jensen began to play the current Number One record, which ironically was *Happy Talk* by Captain Sensible.

"Will you turn that flaming song off?" he shouted and then apologised.

"I'm sorry, Amanda, but it gets on my nerves at the best of times and the one thing that we are not engaging in at the moment is Happy Talk.

"Why end it with me when we've been getting on so well? This Tarquin turns up and you promptly ditch me. Why do you think it will be any different with him this time?"

"I suppose that I thought that I'd got over him, but I hadn't. It's as simple as that. I can't move on until I've got him out of my system."

"Look, Amanda" he replied, trying not to show how desperate he was feeling. "Why don't you and I carry on going out together but if you want to see this character once in a while, then fine. If you decide that he really is the one for you…well, so be it. I'll accept that and back out with grace."

"No, Nigel, that wouldn't be fair on either of you-I've made my mind up and I've got to stick with that decision, whether it's right or wrong."

A gloomy silence descended on them, which was finally broken by Amanda saying: "I think it's best you go before we both end up in tears. I'm really sorry - I never wanted this to happen."

Nigel opened his mouth to argue but then changed his mind and, without looking at her, walked slowly and wordlessly out of the room and down the stairs, as Jane had done a few years before, the words of Elvis Costello's *Good Year For The Roses* playing in his head. He hoped and prayed that she would come running after him, but she did not and he found himself on the street, where he hailed a taxi to take him home.

Back in his own flat, where he played *Positively 4th Street* several times over, enjoying the vitriol which Bob Dylan had obviously poured into the song, before telephoning Pete and Roger to see if either of them could meet him the following night and arranging to meet Roger.

After that, he made the mistake of putting on the television where ITV were showing Simon and Garfunkel's concert in Central Park from the previous summer. He and Amanda had seen them a few weeks previously at Wembley Stadium and hearing the same songs now brought back memories of that wonderful June evening and made him feel completely wretched-particularly a wistful song called *April Come She Will*, all about a love which began in spring, ended in July and, by the time 'autumn winds blow chilly and cold' was no more than a memory.

The words seemed to sum up exactly how he felt, as he tried to explain to Roger the next evening.

"I just feel like I've been had, Rog. I thought it was all going really well…I'd worked out for myself that she'd finished with some bloke not long before she started going out with me but she never mentioned him and I thought he was well and truly off the scene. Now she's back with him-I despair of women, I really do."

"Who is this guy?"

"Somebody she went out with at university and up until a few weeks ago, apparently-rejoices by the name of Tarquin, would you believe?"

"Tarquin? What kind of a name is that?"

"To quote Catch-22, it's Tarquin's name, heaven help him. He sounds a complete prat but he just turns up on her doorstep with a wailing and gnashing of teeth and they're back in lurve and I'm history.

"I just feel like I've been playing a bit part in somebody else's story, like in that Dylan song: *you just kind of wasted my precious time...but don't think twice it's alright.*"

" You don't sound like you're taking it quite so philosophically as Bob.

" I don't know what to say, Nige: I always found that talking to Amanda was like walking on glass but she was gentle with you and I always thought that she was really fond of you."

"At least she's moved to another department now, so that I don't have to see her every day. From now on, I'm giving up on women altogether."

"How many times have I heard you say that? The first time, if my memory serves me well, was at the Freshers' Disco when you spent all evening plying a young nurse with Rum and Black and then her six foot eight, twenty stone rugby-player boyfriend appeared.... In the immortal words of Shakespeare, Exit Troy followed by bear."

"I'd forgotten that one-why do I have this happy knack of picking the no-hopers?"

"I wish I knew, Nige. Same again?"

"Please, Rog."

He wound up drinking 6 or 7 pints of Watneys' Red Barrel - far more than he had been used to drinking in recent years - before rounding the evening off with a curry and it was only when he stumbled to bed that he remembered that he had a Bodkin Manners' Tax Department meeting at 8.30am the following morning.

When he woke, he had a dull aching in his head but managed to eat some breakfast and generally felt rather better than he might have expected.

The journey into the office on a crowded Tube was, however, rather an ordeal and he was feeling distinctly fragile by the start of the department meeting.

The department was headed by Richard Davies, a deceptively benign looking man in his mid-40s with a thinning hair and little round John Lennon glasses. He was generally referred to around the office (though never to his face) as Dickie (after Dickie Davies, the bouffant-haired presenter of ITV's World Of Sport) or Dick Dastardly.

For most of the meeting, Nigel was able to sit quietly without being called upon to contribute, which was just as well as his head was beginning to thump and he was starting to feel decidedly hot and sickly in the airless meeting room. Eventually, however, Dick Dastardly turned to him, smiled weakly and announced:

"I'm now going to ask Nigel to address us on the subject of a new scheme that we have devised which we believe should help to minimise capital gains tax on company sales."

Nigel tried to speak but his mouth began soundlessly to open and close like the Mechanical Fish in Stingray: his throat felt dry, his forehead by now felt cold and clammy and his head was beginning to feel as though it was being struck repeatedly with a blunt axe.

"We have... er... been considering a potential lacuna in the wording of sub-section two of section ..." he began before a wave of nausea overwhelmed him and he just had the presence of mind to turn away from the table and to be sick into the nearest available receptacle, which was the waste paper basket.

"Do apologise.... dodgy curry last night" he muttered before half-walking, half-running out of the room to the men's toilet. He could see looks of horror and sympathy in the eyes of several of his colleagues, while others were clearly enjoying his misfortune and calculating that the chances of his being a rival for partnership were fast receding.

He went straight home and put himself to bed and nothing further was ever said to him about the episode. He soon became aware, however, that his career prospects had been damaged irretrievably - never again was he drafted into the team advising on a high profile deal and he gradually began to see others (many of whom he knew to be less able) promoted ahead of him. From his friends he was able to establish that the story of the waste paper basket incident had reached the higher echelons of the firm and that the word was that there were serious doubts about his professionalism and commitment.

Meanwhile, he had continued successfully to avoid Amanda over the next few weeks and when he finally found himself in close proximity to her, at a leaving do for one of his colleagues at a local hostelry, he ostentatiously remained standing at the bar while she sat at a table with a group of friends.

As the evening wore on, he began to give surreptitious glances in her direction and could sense that she was trying - unsuccessfully - to catch his eye. Gradually, his glances became rather more lengthy and he could see that she was looking extremely unhappy. *Odi et Amo*, he thought to himself, quoting Catullus. I hate and yet I love. It was painful to see her looking so miserable and, eventually, he decided that he was being childish and wandered over to talk to her.

"Hi, Amanda. How've you been?"

"Fine, thanks. What about you?"

"I'm OK. Over-worked and under-paid as usual, you know how it is." She smiled faintly:

"I heard about your, er, gastronomic disorder and your unusual contribution to Dastardly's team meeting. That story seems to have passed into Bodkin Manners folklore."

Nigel laughed: "Bit of a cock-up on the sobriety front, I'm afraid. Glad to know I've made my mark on the legal profession, although I'm not sure that that was the best way to make friends and influence people. I don't exactly seem to be flavour of the month these days - the beard was bad enough, but a bearded dipsomaniac... every time I receive any internal post I expect it to contain my P45.

"Anyhow, that's enough about me. How's Tarquinius Superbus?"

Amanda's face crumpled. "I don't know and I don't care. We fell out again after a couple of weeks - terminally, this time. I've made a real hash of everything, haven't I?"

They wound up going for a curry on Brick Lane, which Nigel thought was a suitably unromantic venue - his first visit there since the night before the morning of the waste paper basket. When the waiter - who knew him from that and many previous visits - asked, "what would your girlfriend like to drink?" he silenced the man by blurting out very loudly "she is not my girlfriend", after which he apologised.

"I'm sorry; it's great to be with you again but it feels very strange. I've missed you terribly."

"I've missed you too" she smiled.

They finished the evening by arranging to go out to the cinema the following week and, somehow, after that, they gradually drifted back into the relationship that they had had before Tarquin's dramatic reappearance on the scene.

"I'm sure that the burning question in the office" he told her one night in an insalubrious steak house on Oxford Street "is what an uptown, up tempo woman like you sees in a downtown, downbeat guy like me."

"I've been wondering that myself" she laughed. "Maybe it's because behind that Little Boy Lost look of yours is someone who's good fun to be with and who's very kind and considerate in his own particular way.

"I like to think as well that you're not the sort of person who just wants me because I go with the image they want to project-I may be wrong, but I feel that you love me for the person I am."

In other words, he thought, my U.S.P. is that I'm not Tarquin. Still, maybe Roger was right and she really is genuinely fond of me...."

"So if I were to ask you to marry me, would I be wasting my time?"

"The only way to find out is to ask, isn't it?"

"Consider yourself asked, then."

"You'll have to do a bit better than that, Nigel."

"Okay, then.... Amanda, will you marry me?"

"I'm sorry, Nigel, but the answer's 'no'" she replied quickly but then, seeing the look of devastation on his face, she took his hand (Boy George and Culture Club were playing in the background, he subsequently recalled).

"Forgive me, Nigel, that was really cruel-my misplaced attempt at humour. Of course the answer is 'yes.' With all thy Bob Dylan records you can me endow."

They married later that year, with Roger (who had spun a coin with Pete for the honour) as best man. Despite the autumnal weather, Amanda wore an off-the shoulder dress and Nigel thought that he had never seen her looking so lovely or so happy.

Matt was conceived early on in their marriage (to the strains of Frankie Goes To Hollywood and Two Tribes, he always maintained) and Amanda, who was already by then beginning to carve out a reputation for herself at Bodkin Manners, enhanced that reputation by working right up until her waters broke - even then, as legend had it, she refused to go to the hospital until she had finished the agreement that she was drafting. It was after she went back to work following her (brief) maternity leave that he began to feel that they were growing apart and that feeling increased after Galadriel was born.

For the first few years the children had been brought up by a succession of nannies, the last of whom, a statuesque blonde from Stockholm, had been sacked after her photograph had been found in various local telephone boxes, touting her wares as Insatiable Ingrid. To add insult to injury, he realised that the number she gave was the number of his mobile, which he had absent-mindedly mislaid a few weeks previously.

As Amanda's reputation as a rain-maker grew and she became first an associate and then a partner, Nigel became more and more disillusioned as it became increasingly obvious that his career was going nowhere and eventually he suggested that he leave private practice and find a lecturing job which would enable him to take more responsibility for looking after the children – a proposal which Amanda accepted with some enthusiasm. Hence his recent career among the Dreaming Spires of Hackney.

In part, he knew, he resented the fact that she had become so successful while he felt that he was still waiting to throw a six to start but he also wished that, just once in a while, she would stop being so "focused" and "driven" (as she was so rapturously described on the appraisal forms that she loved to show him) and go back to being the kookie New Romantic with whom he had fallen in love.

Only very occasionally would her unconventional side resurface - Bodkin Manners normally laid on a karaoke at their annual party and Amanda and a group of other female partners would always get up and sing songs from Grease, calling themselves the Cellulite Sextet-their rendition of *Look At Me, I'm Sandra Dee* had become legendary within the firm and was always eagerly awaited. Sadly, though, even those fleeting moments always seemed to be in a work-related setting - if only she would make time to have some fun just with me once in a while, he often thought.

It had been so different with Sally today: he resolved to see her again, although he had no idea of what he was hoping for by doing so. He would leave it a few days, so as not to make her feel pressurised, and then e-mail her to sound out the prospects for future meetings.

Chapter 10

He managed to control his impatience for a couple of days and then began to compose an e-mail to her. After due consideration, he decided that his opening gambit should be warm and friendly but not too effusive and certainly not overtly romantic.

To: ***Sally Peters***
From: ***Nigel Troy***
It was great to see you again - I hope you enjoyed it as much as I did. Whatever happened to the last however many years?
Nigel

To: ***Nigel Troy***
From: ***Sally Peters***
I really enjoyed myself too. You haven't changed very much at all - I had expected you to be far more world-weary and cynical. Academia obviously suits you.
I hope you thought that I am growing old gracefully (yes, I am fishing for a compliment here!).
Sally

To: ***Sally Peters***
From: ***Nigel Troy***
You looked great. It was strange - we hadn't seen each other in 25 years but just seemed to pick up where we left off.

To: ***Nigel Troy***
From: ***Sally Peters***
We left off with you telling me that you didn't want to see me again, as I recall, so I think it is just as well that we didn't pick up from there....
Sally
Reminding her of how we parted company all those years ago was not

a smart move, Nigel, old son, he thought to himself. He sensed though that the gentle reproach was playful rather than embittered and decided on a reasonably frank-but not unduly defensive-response.

To: **Sally Peters**
From: **Nigel Troy**
Truth to tell, I soon came to regret that decision and have done so ever since.
   Might you be free at any time on Saturday? I hate to sound surreptitious but Amanda is going off on a business trip to Brazil and Matt and Ria seem to lead entirely separate lives from their father, so I will have plenty of time on my hands.
   N

To: **Nigel Troy**
From: **Sally Peters**
Brazil?!

To: **Nigel Troy**
From: **Sally Peters**
Yeah - where the wax come from (sorry!)
   Her firm thinks it's a good idea if the partners in the European offices came together with the partners in the American offices from time to time, to bond in a luxury hotel in an exotic location.
   Actually, a few years ago they had a team-building weekend, which involved being taken out onto the middle of Dartmoor in the depths of winter by some ex-SAS guys and told to fend for themselves with just a box of matches and a ball of twine. Amanda's solution was to bribe said ex-SAS guys to drop her off at a hotel en route - it showed initiative and she became a partner soon after.
   Thankfully, the University doesn't see staff bonding as a priority. Anyhow, Saturday?
   N

To: **Nigel Troy**
From: **Sally Peters**

I think it's best we don't get into the habit of meeting regularly, Nigel. It was great to see you again but it seems wrong somehow to meet as soon as your wife's back is turned.

I had promised myself a visit to the Saatchi Gallery on Saturday....

S.

To: **Sally Peters**
From: **Nigel Troy**

I do understand and don't want to make you feel guilty.

The Saatchi Gallery has been high on my list of things to see for some time - isn't Tracey Emin's unmade bed there?

To: **Nigel Troy**
From: **Sally Peters**

I believe it is - I expect it to look rather like your room in Bateman Street. I will be there around 11.30....

S.

Chapter 11

Sally was already standing in front of Tracey Emin's bed when Nigel arrived. "What do you think?" she asked.

"Well, at least I can understand what it's supposed to be, which is more than I can say for some of the stuff I've seen. To be truthful, I am more of a Raphael and Botticelli man-maybe Monet at a push."

"It's time you moved into the twentieth century-let alone the twenty first. Come on, let's take a proper look round."

She took him by the arm and led him through the gallery. Nigel could tell that she was really enjoying what she saw and, for her benefit, he affected a greater enthusiasm than he really felt.

"What do you make of this, then, Nigel?" she asked, pointing to what to him looked like an amorphous blob of gunge on a canvas. "Don't you think it symbolizes the dichotomy at the very heart of all human existence?"

"Oh, yes, absolutely."

"The essential transience of mankind in a universe which is itself essentially ephemeral?"

"I couldn't have put it better myself."

"Or school custard covered in Iced Gems?"

"Now you come to mention it...to be honest, it looks like it's been painted by Rolf Harris high on LSD."

She laughed: "I think we've had enough culture - fancy some lunch?"

They adjourned to a nearby café and sat at a table next to a party of noisy, but cheerful, German teenagers.

There was no awkwardness between them this time and they soon began to reminisce about their youth in the 1970s.

"We were lucky to be born when we were, weren't we? She asked. " Those were great years to be teenagers. *Et in Arcadia ego.*"

"Bliss it was in that dawn to be alive

But to be young was very heaven."

"Strawbs was that?"

"Keats, wasn't it?"

"Wordsworth, actually, writing about the French Revolution. Wonderful words but I suspect that the bliss might have been somewhat dissipated if you were a young aristocrat en route to an appointment with the guillotine. No danger of that in the seventies, though-Eddie Wareing and Jeux Sans Frontieres was about as aggressive as it got."

"If the alternative was interminable games of It's A Knockout, I think I would probably opt for the executioner's axe but you're quite right, it was a good time to be growing up, although at the time I always felt more than a little short-changed by being born when I was."

"Why was that?"

"It sounds stupid now but as a child I used to feel that I had missed out by not being alive during the war. My parents and all the other oldies always seemed to be talking about the war years and it seemed so glamorous and exciting-particularly in those black and white films that were on television every Sunday evening. That generation also seemed to date everything by whether it happened before, during or after the war and so it seemed to me then like a really special time."

"Maybe they looked back on the war years as a time when normal routine was suspended and they were spared the daily grind?"

"I'm sure that that was it. Okay, you never knew when you or your loved ones might be killed but you probably lived your life in sharper focus than at any other time."

"I can't say I ever felt that my life was any the poorer for being a post-war baby boomer - kipper ties and platform soles may have been the height of bad taste but I think I would have preferred them to swastikas and jackboots any day and ITMA and all that stuff leaves me cold."

"I feel the same now but that's not how I saw it when I were a lad. Missing the war was disappointment enough but the real tragedy was missing out on the Sixties. The Beatles, the Stones, Carnaby Street, Swinging London -it seemed a really vibrant time and I somehow contrived to be just a few years too young to be part of it.

"I always claim that the first single I ever bought was *Purple Haze* by Jimi Hendrix but really it was *Paddy McGinty's Goat* by Val Doonican. Sad, isn't it?"

"I'm afraid that mine was *Mouldy Old Dough* by Lieutenant Pigeon which is probably worse-at least you had the excuse of being a child, whereas I must have been twelve or thirteen, so I was old enough to have known better. I think, though, that people's memories of the sixties are highly selective-everybody thinks of going to San Francisco and wearing flowers in your hair but they forget Junior Choice and all those Pinky and Perky records."

"What about the mouse living in the windmill in Old Amsterdam? Or Lulu singing *I'm A Tiger?*"

"Exactly-and do you remember that one about Grocer Jack?"

"I fear that that may have been in my collection too-*Excerpt From A Teenage Opera* was it's proper title, I believe. I do remember as a small boy listening to my dad's collection of Acker Bilk records and feeling totally underwhelmed and then hearing the Beatles for the first time-*She Loves You* it was, on Three Way Family Favourites. I was completely knocked out by it and there and then I made my mother cancel my subscription to Jack And Jill and get me the NME instead. She was lucky I didn't want to swap my school blazer for an Afghan coat."

"A bloke I work with maintains that the problem with the sixties was that you thought that everybody else was having a better time than you were-he spent his adolescence waiting for the Permissive Society to reach Newport Pagnell but it never did. While the rest of the world was supposedly having a gigantic love-in, he was staying in to watch The Black and White Minstrels and The Billy Cotton Band Show. Maybe the Swinging Sixties only really happened to the likes of Marianne Faithfull and David Bailey."

"They certainly bypassed my parents and the rest of Dudley - it was always a few years behind the rest of the world and so the hippy movement didn't really begin there until about 1972 when the honest burghers of the town began wearing kaftans and calling each other 'man' and saying everything was 'groovy'. So I guess I didn't miss out altogether. Punk didn't hit town until the early 1980s and I like to think that they are all into Altered Images and Orchestral Manoeuvres In The Dark now."

"Did you go to Chitwan when you were in Nepal? You should have done-all the freaks de-camped there from Kathmandu in the seventies and there were plenty of late-flowering hippies to be seen there. I always remember seeing a bloke sitting on a wall and strumming a guitar and singing that Donovan song-you know, the one that goes *'first there is a mountain, then there is no mountain, then there is'*- really tunelessly. Drugged-up to the eyeballs, he looked."

"Simon, my brother, would have loved a place like that-he's convinced that civilisation ended in 1969 and that the high water-mark of popular music was a song called *The Days Of Pearly Spencer*, by some recently-deceased Irishman. His other favourite is *The Captain Of Your Ship* by Reparata and the Delrons-he even called his daughter Reparata."

"That's almost as off-the wall as Galadriel-what is it about you two and naming your daughters?"

"I think it's worse: at least Ria can shorten her name to something vaguely normal. He does make me laugh, though-he plays in a Jefferson Airplane tribute band and sings *White Rabbit* at fiftieth birthdays and the like. If ever you get invited to a Bah Mitzvah anywhere within a twenty-mile radius of Telford, the entertainment will probably be Simon and his fellow ageing hippies. The Grace Slick equivalent is the wife of the local undertaker-not a pretty sight in a mini skirt."

"I'm not sure that Chitwan would be quite ready for that-best he sticks to Telford for the time being."

"Simon is desperate to hang on to his youth as long as possible-definitely Oldest Swinger In Town material. I, on the other hand, can pinpoint the exact moment when I entered middle age."

"When was that? When you started eyeing up the cardigans and tartan slippers in Littlewoods?"

"No. It happened about 10 years ago. I was sitting in a Beefeater restaurant with the children somewhere between here and my parents' house and found myself tapping my feet to the music that was playing in the background and telling them that they didn't write songs like that any more.... And then I realised the enormity of what was happening: I liked Cliff Richard."

"I'm not sure that that's irrebuttable proof of having entered your dotage-I quite like Cliff."

"It was proof enough for me-I can never hear *The Day I Met Marie* without being reminded of the moment I realised that my youth was gone."

Sally laughed. "I'm still not convinced. My brother reckons that the test of whether you are middle aged in 2003 is whether you are old enough to remember where you were when you heard that President Kennedy had been assassinated. Do you pass that test?"

"I'm not sure whether this means that I am passing or failing, but I can't quite remember hearing the news, although perversely I do remember hearing that a man called Oswald had been shot and my father explaining that he was the man who had shot the President. I have also got a very vivid memory of when Churchill died-it was a Sunday morning and when my father turned on the radio they were playing sombre music on the Light Programme instead of the usual grim muzac that used to get played in those days. At least it meant that the house was a Pinky And Perky -free zone for a few days."

"It was like that when Princess Diana died: I put the radio on for Alistair Cooke and instead it was just funereal music, so I checked the teletext and that was how I found out."

"I heard the news from Amanda who heard it from a taxi driver on her way home from an Amanda Special-a completion meeting which began on Friday and ended in the early hours of Sunday morning."

"It was strange that it was that week, when the news was given over entirely to Diana, that Mother Teresa slipped out of the world-no state funerals, no fuss, she didn't get more than a by-line in the papers. I'm sure that that was significant somehow."

"I guess she wouldn't have wanted it any other way-she must have been a remarkable woman."

"Can you remember when you heard that John Lennon had died?"

"I can: I heard it from John Timpson on the *Today* programme, just as I was getting out of bed-with the mother of all hangovers, if I recall. I can remember when I heard that George Harrison had died too- I read it on a news placard outside Baker Street Tube station and I went home and played *All Things Must Pass* as a tribute. What about you?"

"I can't remember when George died but I was at Uni when Lennon died: none of us had radios so we heard the news from a lecturer who was a real ageing hippy. He broke down in tears and had to give us the morning off, so if I hadn't been a big Beatles fan before that, I always have been since."

"I loved the Beatles but I thought they lost it towards the end: *She's*

Leaving Home was just a dirge and I got irritated by that stupid cow who sang Ob-La-Di Ob-La-Da at every significant moment in her life and had a couple of kids running in the yard within a couple of years of meeting some guy in the market place.

"*Imagine* always irritates me, too-the most over-rated song ever in my book. How much more twee could you get?"

"It is pretty corny, I agree. 'Imagine there's no heaven…. Imagine all the people living for today' is all fine if you are a multimillionaire ex-Beatle and one of the most famous men on the planet, but it doesn't hold out much hope if you are living in grinding poverty in Bangladesh and dreading the arrival of the next cyclone."

"My thoughts exactly."

"The silliest of all though was the bloke in *Twenty Four Hours From Tulsa* who went into the café, put a record on the jukebox and next thing he's telling the waitress he'd die before he let her out of his arms and telling his wife that he won't be coming home any more."

"Yeah-it would be nice to think that she wrote back to say that that was cool because she had already decided to leave him for the milkman. Anyhow, I can safely say that I have long grown out of feeling wistful over the sixties-I loved the heavy rock of the early seventies and, besides, if I'd been there during the sixties, I'd be fast approaching my sell-by date by now."

"And you might have missed Strawbs altogether."

"Just imagine if the soundtrack of my university years had been *Stars On 45*…or Bros."

"Thankfully Bros and Jason Donovan weren't big in Calcutta-maybe that's why I stayed there so long."

"I always remember listening to the Top 20 on the radio on a Sunday evening - banished to my bedroom because my dad wanted to watch Stars on Sunday. There was always plenty of good stuff mixed up with the dross - and then it would come to an end and Sing Something Simple would come on. For me, the Monday morning blues used to begin when I heard that awful music and they started to murder some good songs. The Cliff Adams Singers Play Black Sabbath's Greatest Hits-vomit!

"The other grim point was 5 o'clock on a winter Saturday evening; Wolves would always have lost and Grandstand would be followed by

Bruce Forsyth's Generation Game, with Brucie making fun of some hapless mother and son from Leighton Buzzard while Anthea did endless twirls…. although I have to admit that I rather fancied Anthea at the time."

"My low spot was always when The Golden Shot ended - my parents thought it was too low-brow but I had a big crush on Bernie The Bolt, so we used to argue about whether I could watch it or not. It was the same with Love Thy Neighbour".

Nigel was silent for a few moments then he turned to her: "I'm not just saying this but it has always been one of my big regrets that you and I stopped seeing each other-you've always been my biggest What If? And seeing you again now just seems to reinforce that feeling."

After a brief silence, she said quietly "Maybe you think that because we broke up before things started to turn sour and before we slipped into the same old dull routine."

"It wouldn't necessarily have turned sour."

"Being realistic, Nigel, the chances are that it would have ended anyway and that it would have ended badly but now I remind you of golden days at Cambridge and dancing in the snow-it might be different if you associated me with long winter evenings in front of George and Mildred and Saturday morning trips to IKEA."

"Perhaps. All I know is that it's been great to see you again and I haven't felt so relaxed in anybody's company for a long time. By way of information only, by the way, you have just done what you accuse me of doing-that bit about the same old dull routine comes straight from that song about the guy who tries to run away from his wife and drink Pina Coladas. Plagiarism must be contagious."

They chatted on for some time until Nigel announced that he had better go and see whether Galadriel was up and about yet.

"Can we do this again?" he asked as they left the café.

"I'm sure we can-let's try and find something a bit more Troy-friendly next time, though. Any Strawbs concerts coming up?"

"Sadly not: they do get together for a tour every so often, but there's nothing coming up that I know of. It's a pity-they're a great bunch and after their concerts they hang around and chat and sign CDs. You'd love it."

"Does that mean that I would get to meet the man who wrote that song I really liked?"

"*Angel Wine*? That was written by Chas Cronk and he left the band years ago: they still play it, though."

"Oh, well, do let me know if they ever play any dates in Ealing."

She hesitated. "Nigel, there is one thing I think I should tell you. I do have a loose sort of attachment; to call him a boyfriend is over-stating it and anyway I think we are a bit long in the tooth for that, but he's a guy I used to teach with, called Colin. He's a widower, a few years older than me. We do see quite a lot of each other and he has asked me to marry him a couple of times-it's become almost like a standing invitation.

"I've always said no-or, to be more precise, I've never said yes- but sometimes I wonder if it might be the best thing for me to do. I don't love him but he's good company and kind to me and we have a lot in common. "

"But how can you think of marrying him if you don't love him?"

"Oh, we're not exactly Love's Young Dream but is that really the be-all and end-all? No doubt it was all hearts and flowers between you and Amanda to start with (sorry, that was a mean thing to say). We're good friends and we get on well-wouldn't that be a pretty good start? Maybe I would come to love him-but would it be the end of the world if I didn't?"

"I guess I'm just an incurable romantic, but I think there needs to be a bit of a spark at the beginning, even if it gets put out after a time.

"I do know, though, that it's your life and none of my business, before you tell me that."

"I wouldn't be so rude-bye, Nigel, I've had a lovely time."

Chapter 12

He had planned to wait for a few days before contacting her again but when he checked his mailbox the following Monday evening, he was thrilled to see that Sally had already e-mailed him.

To: Nigel Troy
From: Sally Peters
Hi, Nigel, how was the rest of your weekend? I hope you remained suitably uplifted by the modern art....

To: Sally Peters
From: Nigel Troy
It was ok, thanks. Ria had just surfaced when I got in.
Do you remember The Munsters on TV? Ria reminds me of a young version of the mother (Lily, I think her name was-played by someone called Yvonne de Carlo).
It grieves me that we spend a fortune on a private education for her and then she walks round looking like the sort of thing you'd find on a mortician's slab.
The son and heir is the opposite-one of those healthy rugger b---er types. Cambridge was full of them.
So much for the fruit of my loins-what about you? Busy week?
N

To: Nigel Troy
From: Sally Peters
It is quite a busy time for me-school exams coming up.
Do you ever give your daughter a hard time over how she looks? If you did and if I were her I would dig out some old photos of you from the seventies-pots and kettles and all that!
Is your ever-loving back from Brazil?
S

His face clouded over on reading the reference to Amanda, which made him think that she was deliberately putting up a barrier between them.

To: Sally Peters
From: Nigel Troy

If you mean Amanda, yes, she got back into the country yesterday afternoon and went straight into the office.

Poor Amanda: she has this unbearable young assistant called James who is incredibly keen to impress her with his dedication to the job by working even longer hours than her-if that is humanly (or inhumanly) possible.   He never seems to have a life.

But... Amanda got home comparatively early last night and then had a call from one of the other partners to say that he had caught young James in flagrante delicto across his desk with one of the trainee solicitors. Amanda flew into one of her rages and phoned the unfortunate Jas. in a foul temper telling him that he was for the high jump and could pick up his P45 tomorrow-not because he had been involved in extra-curricular nookie in the office but because he was supposed to have been working late on an urgent deal and this, according to her, proved that he was just a dilettante at heart.

To round it all off, either he or said trainee seems to have knocked his keyboard during the throes of passion and somehow contrived to have deleted the document that they had been working on for weeks.

I haven't stopped laughing all day-for the last few years this James has been held out to me as a young man with all the qualities that I lack and now it transpires that he has not been driven so much by the work ethic as by more... er... carnal desires.

She has always said that he is one of the few young lawyers who is not dead from the neck up - it seems like there are a few twitches of life from the waist down as well!

Anyhow, poor wretch now has an appointment with the Grim Reaper first thing in the morning...

Yours uncharitably.........
Nigel

To: Nigel Troy
From: Sally Peters
Poor chap-couldn't he have maintained that while the partners were team-building in exotic climes he was just doing a bit of bonding of his own…?
What is it my (Business School graduate) brother calls it-horizontal integration?
And who is the Grim Reaper??
S

To: Sally Peters
From: Nigel Troy
The Grim Reaper is the office nickname for the Bodkin Manners managing partner, Robert Watson-a dour Scot who was a contemporary of mine at Cambridge, in fact.
He got the name as a result of a particularly vicious bloodletting exercise which he initiated and which resulted in the culling of nearly a quarter of the partners in the firm, including the parfait, gentle Sir Thomas Manners Bt. who was the grandson of the founder of the firm.
The poor old buffer missed the partners' meeting when these decisions were taken (a long weekend's salmon fishing in Scotland) and received the news by voice mail.
To make it worse, he had no idea how to operate voice mail and had to get his secretary to retrieve the message for him.
The final victory of the Players over the Gentlemen was how my pal Mike Castaldo described it but I prefer to think of it as the night the lunatics took over the asylum.
The rest of the offices are open plan, but the Reaper apparently has this palatial room with leather chairs and carpets four inches thick-universally known as Gestapo Headquarters.
Not a nice man.

To: Nigel Troy
From: Sally Peters
What is happening to the girl?

111

To: **Sally Peters**
From: Nigel Troy
She is due to be reaped at the same time....
The next day, still drunk on Schadenfreude, he e-mailed Mike Castaldo to gloat.

To: **Mike Castaldo**
From: Nigel Troy
Hi, Mike. How're you doing?
Amanda was telling me how the saintly young James (her assistant) was caught (literally) with his trousers down in the office - have you heard the story? Made me laugh.
Best regards.
Nigel

To: **Nigel Troy**
From: Mike Castaldo
Hi, Nigel.
Have I heard the story? Of course I have - there hasn't been so much amusement in the office since ....er ....er... the day of your technicolour yawn, to be precise.
Decent of your missus to save his bacon in the end, wasn't it?
Regards.
Mike

To: **Mike Castaldo**
From: Nigel Troy
Save his bacon? I hadn't heard that.

To: **Nigel Troy**
From: Mike Castaldo
She is alleged to have interceded on his behalf with the Grim Reaper.
Apparently, she persuaded him to drop the charge of intra-office fornication in exchange for a plea of guilty to the lesser charge of contravening the firm's "clean desk" policy by leaving on said desk, between the hours of sunset and sunrise, one item of ladies' underwear

(black) (hereinafter called "the Thong") in contravention of sub-paragraph (k) of paragraph 7 of Chapter 4 of the Bodkin Manners' staff handbook (2002 revision). The sentence for which is apparently a written warning (and a request from the Grim Reaper for the lady's phone number, I rather suspect).

Exhibit A (the Thong) is rumoured to be held in the office safe in case it is ever needed as evidence in future legal proceedings.

Actually, much of this may be apocryphal, but it is true that he escaped with a written warning.

Mike

To: Mike Castaldo
From: Nigel Troy
What about the girl? Presumably what's sauce for the goose....
N

To: Nigel Troy
From: Mike Castaldo
Yes, apparently she (Portia by name!) was reprieved too. One rumour that is currently circulating is that said Portia got a splinter in a very painful place from James' desk and was threatening a personal injury claim.

The other theory is that she has been taking to a fellow trainee, by the name of Belinda - have your heard about Belinda?

To: Mike Castaldo
From: Nigel Troy
No, should I have done??

To: Nigel Troy
From: Mike Castaldo
Doesn't your wife tell you anything?

This Belinda has (allegedly) been supplementing the pittance we pay her by working as a pole dancer in some sleazy Soho strip joint and the Grim Reaper has found out.

BUT he has not been able to take any action - care to guess why not?

To: Mike Castaldo
From: Nigel Troy
I can't imagine!
Because she's been entertaining clients of the firm there and so it counts as marketing?

To: Nigel Troy
From: Mike Castaldo
Good answer, Nigel and in the right ball park but it's better than that.
I'll have to switch over to my Hotmail account-careless talk and all that.

To: Nigel Troy
From: Mike Castaldo-Home
The Reaper found out because he saw her there - he's a regular customer (allegedly).

To: Mike Castaldo-Home
From: Nigel Troy
No way! The Reaper?

To: Nigel Troy
From: Mike Castaldo-Home
The same.
He had been leaving the office comparatively early every Wednesday, saying that he was going to rehearsals for some choir he is in - but it turned out that he was sneaking off to Soho with the dirty raincoat brigade.
He recognised this Belinda - although she was (allegedly) dressed up as a French maid at the time - and she recognised him but they have an unspoken pact that neither will say anything about the episode in the office. In the Cold War it used to be called Mutually Assured Destruction.

To: Mike Castaldo-Home
From: Nigel Troy

Brilliant! But how come the office rumour mill has got hold of the story?

To: Nigel Troy
From: Mike Castaldo-Home
Said Belinda had too much to drink one night and told a couple of fellow trainees... in strictest confidence, of course.
They told a couple of other people ...... also in strictest confidence ...... and it seems like the only person the story hadn't reached was Robert himself - for obvious reasons.
It may have done now though, thanks to young Portia.

To: Mike Castaldo-Home
From: Nigel Troy
Superb. Am I right in thinking that Amanda's other acolyte, the not-quite-so-obnoxious Greg, is cock-a-hoop?

To: Nigel Troy
From: Mike Castaldo-Home
Absolutely. He and a group of fellow upwardly mobile young bucks start whistling Air On A G String every time J appears.
But Greg is skating on thin ice after the fire escape episode.

To: Mike Castaldo-Home
From: Nigel Troy
The fire escape episode?

To: Nigel Troy
From: Mike Castaldo-Home
You haven't heard that one? What do you and Amanda talk about?

To: Mike Castaldo-Home
From: Nigel Troy
We don't talk!!
Spill the beans ......

To: Nigel Troy
From: Mike Castaldo-Home

A couple of years ago they had a big presentation in the office when Halitosis Hilda was finally put out to grass after a century of service (or whatever it was - the old battle-axe should have been shot years ago, if you ask me).

Anyhow, while everyone was assembled to watch the Reaper presenting the old trout with her gold watch, G was being filmed by the security cameras frolicking out on the fire escape with a lady of advancing years and repellent aspect (Barbara by name) from the photocopying department. This Barbara's wardrobe has always been Woman At Asda but the video reveals that underneath the cardigans and sensible skirts it's pure Ann Summers - I know all this because Ron, the security man, was offering private viewings for a modest fee.

To: Mike Castaldo-Home
From: Nigel Troy

It must have been a bit nippy on the fire escape.

To: Nigel Troy
From: Mike Castaldo-Home

Nippy and dangerous!

Anyhow, NT, can't spend all day gossiping - must get my nose back to the grindstone.

See you soon, I hope.

Best regards.

Mike.

He was still laughing to himself as he forwarded the entire exchange of e-mails to Sally.

To: Sally Peters
From: Nigel Troy

The attached may amuse!

I guess I'm glad that James didn't get the old heave-ho in the end - fun to think of him squirming with embarrassment though...

To: Nigel Troy
From: Sally Peters
I thought law firms were serious places of business - this sounds more like Sodom & Gomorrah!

To: Sally Peters
From: Nigel Troy
I am amazed at this sudden outbreak of naughtiness and humour among the earnest young men of Bodkin Manners.
I was sure that they did not have a Human Resources department any more, just a lab in their basement where they clone their young lawyers- the male ones at any rate.   They are all slightly built, prematurely balding with glasses and earnest expressions and they all talk the same -everything is either a "deal stopper" or a "no brainer."
I just assumed that it had been decided that it was far too expensive to give them any sort of personality and so they didn't try.
Makes me glad to be an academic...although my students put a different meaning on the term "no brainer"....
N

To: Nigel Troy
From: Sally Peters
Did you ever see the film Sliding Doors?   I wonder if there is a parallel universe out there where you carried on working as a solicitor and submitted yourself to a personality by-pass in order to get a partnership....
S

After some soul-searching, he decided that perhaps the time was right to introduce a little gentle flirtation into their exchanges and sent a message which he hoped might encourage their virtual conversations to take a more personal turn.

To: Sally Peters
From: Nigel Troy
Maybe there is a parallel universe where you and I carried on going

out together....
N

To: Nigel Troy
From: Sally Peters
*Perhaps-containing a scrap yard with the remains of a Ford Capri,
with 'Nige' and 'Sal' on the sun strip???*
S

A humorous but very 'safe' response, he thought-and decided to
respond in the same vein.

To: Sally Peters
From: Nigel Troy
*Unlikely. I'm sure you could buy those sun strips with any girl's name
you liked, as long as it was Tracey.*
*Anyway I never ran to a Ford Capri-my first car was a Citroen 2CV
which did nought-to- sixty in three months.*
*Amanda has a Porsche (ACT 1) which does nought- to- sixty in one
nanosecond but I don't think it has ever got out of first gear as she only
ever drives round London.*
Where are you going on holiday this year?
N

To: Nigel Troy
From: Sally Peters
*I had an expensive holiday last summer (6 weeks in India) so I'm not
going anywhere this year-mainly staying in London, although I will
spend a week or so with my parents in Cambridge.*
What about you?

To: Sally Peters
From: Nigel Troy
*Nothing planned. The children don't want to come with us anymore-
Mat is off on a Club 18-30 holiday on a Greek island and Ria doesn't
seem to have the energy or enthusiasm to go anywhere. Amanda's idea
of the perfect holiday destination is somewhere where she can use her*

laptop and her mobile and with a short flight home if anything urgent crops up at the office, so we mainly just go on (not very) long weekend breaks to European cities.

Ideally she likes to go wherever her firm has an office so that she can check them out and "kick ass" if she concludes that they are not coming up to scratch (which she normally does).

Meanwhile I do some sightseeing-the arrangement works quite well.

Would prefer Club 18-30 though....

To: **Nigel Troy**
From: Sally Peters
The problem is that we are both at that difficult age-too old for 18-30, too young for Saga...

To: **Sally Peters**
From: Nigel Troy
Don't forget that it's the generation who were young in the sixties who are eligible for Saga holidays now, so maybe they have geriatric love-ins before their cocoa...

I often listen to Saga Radio-only place where you get to hear Led Zeppelin!

But how do the crumblies play air guitar <u>and</u> hold onto their Zimmer frames?

N

To: **Nigel Troy**
From: **Sally Peters**
You'll be telling me you listen to the Archers next....

To: **Sally Peters**
From: **Nigel Troy**
Absolutely - it's pretty raunchy stuff these days.
Anyhow, I still feel like a 19-year old... given half a chance anyway!
N

To: *Nigel Troy*
From: *Sally Peters*
That was sooo predictable, that one!
S
From: *Nigel Troy*

To: *Sally Peters*
Sorry.
Seriously, though, it is weird-I look out on the world with the same eyes as when I was 19 and don't feel very different-except that such faculties as I ever had are slowly but inexorably being lost.

Sometimes, I think I might grow the beard back-do you realise that I spend 8 minutes per day shaving?

That makes 56 minutes a week.

Which is about 28 minutes a month.

So I waste about 6 hours a year shaving.

So if I live another 60 years (a distinct possibility), I will spend one of those years shaving-it beggars belief.

To: *Nigel Troy*
From: *Sally Peters*
Forgive me for lowering the tone, but think how many of those years you are going to be spending on the loo!

To: *Sally Peters*
From: *Nigel Troy*
Good point, Sally.
On that subject, the attached e-mail was circulating around Amanda's firm a few weeks ago.

To: *All Partners and Staff*
From: *The Managing Partner*
The partners have recently engaged a firm of management consultants to advise on how we can increase our profitability and one of the issues highlighted in their report is the amount of time spent by staff in the lavatory and its impact on our financial performance.

They found that, on average, each individual visits the lavatory 4 times a day and that each trip (including time spent walking to and from the lavatory) takes an average of 5 minutes.

That means that each fee earner spends an average of 20 minutes each working day in the aptly named rest rooms and so 600 fee earners spend a total of 200 chargeable hours a day answering calls of nature.

At an average charge-out rate of £400 per hour, a staggering £80,000 of fee income is literally being flushed down the pan every day.

If this were to go straight onto the bottom line, it would give additional profits per equity partner of £100,000.

This cannot be allowed to continue and, with immediate effect, the firm will be monitoring visits to the WC: I will personally be patrolling the floors with a clipboard and stopwatch and noting the amount of time each person spends in the toilet.

In due course, we propose to install (hands-free) digital dictation equipment with voice-recognition software in all cubicles, but until then I expect "Number Ones" to take no more than 2 minutes and "Number Twos" no more than 3 minutes. Failure to observe these time limits will be treated as a disciplinary offence.

Anyone found reading (other than the Law Society's Gazette and other legal periodicals) or sending text messages in/from the toilets will be summarily dismissed.

Robert Watson (Managing Partner)

To: Nigel Troy
From: Sally Peters
Very funny, Nigel. Presumably it was a spoof?

To: Sally Peters
From: Nigel Troy
Apparently so-Mike sent it to me and I suspect that he may have been the author.

*They are always bringing in so-called experts who charge them a small fortune for stating the ******* obvious though.*

Those mentioned in the e-mail sound like time and motion consultants (geddit?).

Anyhow, enough of all this lavatorial humour -I was wondering if you would like to go and see a film one night. I haven't been to the cinema for years and it would be fun.

N

To: **Nigel Troy**
From: **Sally Peters**
That would be really nice. When?

To: **Sally Peters**
From: **Nigel Troy**
This sounds awfully clandestine and I apologise in advance but how about Wednesday?

Amanda is going to the opera with clients that night and so my absence won't be noticed (not that it ever is....)

N

To: **Nigel Troy**
From: **Sally Peters**
I am afraid that meeting like this still makes me feel more than a little guilty but OK, let's make it Wednesday.

What would you like to see?

To: **Sally Peters**
From: **Nigel Troy**
Don't mind - your choice.

? Oxford Circus Tube Station at (?)6.30pm, so that we can grab a bite to eat first?

To: **Nigel Troy**
From: **Sally Peters**
OK. I will see you there - by ticket office....

To: **Sally Peters**
From: **Nigel Troy**

Look forward to it.

To: Nigel Troy
From: Sally Peters
Great.
S x

Chapter 13

Throughout that Wednesday Nigel felt a tremendous thrill of excitement as he looked forward to spending the evening with Sally. There was a delightful innocence about going to the cinema, which made him feel like a teenager about to embark on his first date. Even a two-hour afternoon lecture on the fascinating subject of "depreciatory transactions under the Income and Corporation Taxes Act 1988" failed to dispel his good humour and he smiled benignly on his students throughout the session, even managing the occasional witticism - quite a feat, given the dry nature of the subject-matter.

He was just about to leave the university in good time to meet Sally when the telephone rang - it was Amanda.

"Hello, Nigel, it's me. You haven't forgotten that we're going to Fidelio tonight, have you?"

"Nigel's heart sank. "I knew you were going to the opera tonight, but I'm not included am I?"

"Of course you are, you idiot, we are going with Barry Morton and his wife - you didn't think I was going to play gooseberry with the two of them, did you?

"You'll have to go home and change - I'm going straight from the office, so I'll see you in the foyer at 7.15."

He tried to argue but Amanda was not in the mood for debate.

"I've got a client holding for me and my mobile's going as well - don't be late. And be polite to Barry."

With that, she put the receiver down, leaving Nigel aghast at the thought of having to cancel his evening with Sally and at the prospect of having to spend it in the company of Barry Morton.

Barry was chief executive of one of Amanda's most prestigious clients - a big, bulldog of a man with (Nigel thought) the distinct air of a bully. Nigel had met him once before and had taken an instant dislike to him.

His first priority, he knew, was to telephone Sally to give his apologies and try to rearrange the cinema trip but, to his horror, he realised that he did not have a phone number for her or even her address to enable him to get the number from Directory Enquiries. He did however have her e-mail address so he dashed off a quick e-mail to her and hoped that she would see it in time:

Sally, so sorry - last minute problem. Will have to cancel tonight. Just hope you get this before you leave for the West End. My apologies again.

Nigel

He then took the Tube home and did a quick change into the blazer and grey flannel trousers that he normally wore on smart social occasions, before taking a taxi to Covent Garden. After a time, he gave up tormenting himself by imagining Sally spending the evening alone at Oxford Circus and began to speculate what Mrs Morton would be like. The archetypal Essex woman, he decided, called Chardonnay or something of that ilk (the one programme he watched on television, apart from repeats of Fawlty Towers and Blackadder, was Footballers Wives) and wearing even more gold jewellery than her husband, if that was possible.

He arrived at Covent Garden just a moment or two after the appointed time and rushed into the foyer where, to his horror, he realised that all the other men (Barry included) were wearing black tie. Amanda gave him one of her just-wait-till-I-get-you-home looks while he mumbled his apologies and embarked on a story about how his dinner suit had been unavoidably detained at the dry cleaners.

Eventually he pulled himself together and, remembering that he had been given strict instructions by Amanda to conceal his dislike of Barry, greeted him with an energetic handshake and a cheery "Hi, Bazza, good to see you again", which brought a hissed "call him Barry, you imbecile" from Amanda.

Barry returned the greeting cordially enough and then introduced them to his wife, who turned out to be called Jean and not at all what Nigel had expected. She was a rather shy and gentle-looking soul, with bobbed grey hair and surprisingly little make-up or jewellery. She gave the impression that she had been told to speak only when spoken to and, as Amanda and Barry completely monopolised the conversation with an animated discussion about the progress of Barry's latest deal, that meant that she kept almost total silence during the twenty minutes or so that they spent in the bar before the performance.

Eventually he turned to her and made the comment that had been in his thoughts since they were first introduced:

"Jean Morton? Wasn't that the name of the presenter of Tingha and Tucker?"

He immediately regretted the comment as Jean seemed to be the sort of person who was unlikely to do humour but, to his surprise, she laughed heartily.

"That dates you, Nigel. It was only after Barry and I got married that I realised that I was destined to spend the rest of my life bringing back memories of Willy Wombat and Katie Kookaburra. I might well have had second thoughts if I'd known beforehand."

"Well it could have been a lot worse - we had a master at school who rejoiced by the name of Basil Brush - I kid you not. He was a hatched-faced old goat - not the sort to punctuate his lessons with the odd 'boom! boom!'".

The sound of his (very passable) impersonation of the famous fox brought another withering look from Amanda, who then proceeded to usher them all towards their seats.

Afterwards they adjourned to a nearby Italian restaurant where Barry condescended to address Nigel for the first time since they had shaken hands.

"I gather you were at Bodkin Manners, Nigel, before you opted for academic life. What was the big attraction? The holidays? "

"No, I'm afraid that they decided that I didn't have what it takes - to be more precise, I disgraced myself by throwing up in a wastepaper basket during a meeting."

Barry looked momentarily nonplussed, Amanda glared but, to his surprise, Jean gave another cheery laugh.

Barry immediately began to tell a long and, in Nigel's opinion, extremely un-funny story about their attempts to move house ("you can't get anything half decent in Kent for under two million can you?") and the problems he had encountered with the small, high street firm of solicitors who were acting for their vendors. To Nigel's irritation, Amanda seemed to be hanging on to his every word and braying with laughter in a very affected way every time he said anything that he obviously thought was funny (which was most of the time).

He perked up, however, when their main courses arrived and took advantage of a momentary pause in Barry's monologue to make a quip at the expense of the waiter:

"It makes me laugh when these effeminate little waiters come round brandishing their enormous pepper mills- Freud would have a field day with them. I'm sure it's just to try to convince themselves-and us-of their own masculinity.

"It's the same with those Japanese tourists, with their massive zoom lenses" he ploughed on, warming to his theme, until he was silenced by Amanda's glare which (to quote the Eagles) was chilly enough to make hell freeze over.

He could see Barry giving her a pitying look but, to his surprise, Jean gave a loud guffaw and announced: " I must remember that theory. Perhaps it explains why my husband likes to drive round London in a huge Land Cruiser" – after which it was Barry's turn to fix his spouse with a chilly stare before he changed the subject abruptly and began to give his verdict on the evening's performance.

"Workmanlike rather than inspired, I would say. I thought the bloke who played Fidelio was a bit out of tune at times and the soprano seemed to be having trouble hitting some of the high notes. What did you think, Mand?"

"I thought the music was wonderful" Nigel interjected "but couldn't understand how prisoners who had spent years living on a starvation diet were all built like brick privies. Same with La Boheme: there's Mimi on her death-bed, dying of consumption, yet she manages to belt out a five minute aria with what's supposed to be her dying breath."

"Nigel's idea of culture is listening to Bob Dylan," commented Amanda dismissively.

"I'm with you on that Nigel" said Jean, rather unexpectedly. "I'm a great Dylan fan."

"Oh really?" he asked, perking up again. "How come?"

She smiled.

"I've got a brother who's a few years older than me and he was always playing Dylan records - so it was almost osmosis with me. When I was at junior school we had a Christmas party and we were all allowed to bring one record in: all the other children bought *Lily The Pink* but I turned up with *Stuck Inside Of Mobile With The Memphis Blues Again.*"

"I bet that went down well," he laughed.

"It did actually - our teacher had well and truly overdosed on Pink Old Lily filling up with paraffin inside and so *Stuck Inside of Mobile* must have come as a welcome relief."

"So what's your favourite Dylan album?"

"I love the classics from the sixties, like *Blonde on Blonde and Highway* 61."

"And your favourite song?"

"That's hard-either *Queen Jane Approximately* or *Sad-Eyed Lady Of the Lowlands,* I think. What about you?"

"I remember hearing *The Times They Are A-Changin'*" on Top Of The Pops and thinking his voice was the worst I had ever heard, so I forgot all about him until I went to university and got to know the guy in the room next door who was a complete Dylan freak and turned me onto *Blood On The Tracks.* So I think that's my favourite, closely followed by *Desire, which came out during me second term.*"

"So you're not so keen on the 'sixties albums?"

"I've got to know them over the years and they're wonderful, but they were already classics and those two are the ones that bring back memories for me and the ones I like the most. I guess that it's like John Lennon said-it's all about 'being here now.'"

"I liked *Street Legal* too - and *Slow Train,* but I gave up on him after that and just listen to the older stuff now - when Barry lets me, that is."

"You should get the two most recent albums - they've been a real return to form. Have you ever seen him live?"

"Yes, a few times - I saw him at Earls Court in the late seventies, then at Blackbush and again a couple of years after that but Barry can't stand him unfortunately, so I haven't been to see him since."

"I was at Earls Court, too. We queued up a whole weekend to get tickets. I think I've seen him on most tours since then. The last time - a couple of years ago - was one of the best. He's coming to London again in November - I'll be going with a group of friends who are fellow

Dylan buffs."

They carried on in this vein for the rest of the evening, while Barry and Amanda ignored them completely - at one point Nigel could see Amanda smiling broadly as Barry enthused about how she had run rings around the hapless senior partner of a firm from Stoke-On-Trent and, later, to his total mortification, the room fell silent just as Amanda was extolling the virtues of colonic irrigation to Barry, who gave every appearance of being totally fascinated by the subject.

"Puts you off your food, doesn't it?" he muttered to Jean, who smiled conspiratorially.

"I hope she doesn't persuade Barry to try it: I'm sure he would be a mere shadow of his former self afterwards, he's so full of, er, his own importance."

"Look, Jean" Nigel said eventually, as Amanda was settling the bill, "you're very welcome to come with us to the Dylan concert, if you can stand the thought of spending an evening in the company of a bunch of anoraks from a third division university."

"Thank you, Nigel. I'd love to come-and I can't think of any way I'd rather spend an evening than with a bunch of Dylan nuts. It would make a welcome change from captains of industry."

"That's great then: I haven't got round to buying the tickets yet but I'll do it in the next week or so. It's a Thursday night and I'm pretty sure it's the twelfth of November but I'll check and let you know via Amanda and Barry. We can firm up the arrangements nearer the time."

"Wonderful-I feel really excited about it already. I never thought I'd get to see the great man again. Thanks for asking me-it's been lovely meeting you...and Amanda too."

"Well, Nigel" said Amanda when they were on their way home in their taxi, you're a total embarrassment but you deserve a medal for keeping that boring cow amused."

Although tempted to bask in the glow of this unaccustomed praise, Nigel felt honour-bound to stand up for Jean. "She wasn't boring at all - she's a nice lady and interesting company. Her problem is that nobody takes any time to find out what she's all about - least of all her loud-mouthed bully of a husband."

Nigel paused to make sure that Amanda had not recognised that some of his words were in fact lifted from a Byrds' song called *Old John Robertson* and then continued.

"Honestly, Amanda, I don't know how you can fall all over that bloke, laughing hysterically at his attempts at humour and hanging on his every word."

"Well, at least he's a deal-doer and a wealth-creator - better that than being a chronic under-achiever with no career and no prospects."

Stung by those words - which he knew were unerringly accurate - he hesitated for a moment to give himself chance to think of a suitably witty reply before retorting: "Well, I'd rather be a chronic under-achiever with no career and no prospects than ... a loud mouthed git."

Feeling ashamed of the weakness of his riposte, he cast around for something with which to wound her, before adding: "If you gave as much time and attention to your husband and your children as you give to people like him, we might be a less dysfunctional family."

Even in the darkness of the cab, he knew that she was glaring at him.

"So that's what all this is about, is it?"

"All what's about?"

"You really resent the fact that I've got a successful career, don't you?"

"That's absurd, Amanda."

"It isn't, it's the truth. Well, let me remind you that it was you who suggested that you go into lecturing: I was very happy with that decision as it seemed to make a lot of sense but if you'd wanted to carry on as a lawyer, I would've gone along with that and would have found a way of organizing my life to fit in with yours. We'd have had plenty of money for nannies or whatever but you've never shown the slightest sign of wanting to go back into private practice-even when tax lawyers have been as hard to find as rocking horse manure. I'm sorry but you can't have it both ways-you haven't got an ounce of drive in your body, have you?"

They spent the rest of the journey in stony silence and that continued until they were home and in bed, when Amanda was the first to wave an olive branch.

"I'm sorry - that comment of mine was below the belt. I know that Barry is full of himself and not a particularly nice bloke but there aren't the corporate deals around at the moment, so clients like Barry who are still out there in the market trying to do deals are like gold dust. If I don't keep him sweet, he'll go somewhere else and if that happened... well, nobody's indispensable. Life has changed since you were in the profession - the world doesn't owe anybody a living any more.

"I haven't sold my soul, Nigel, I promise - but sometimes I feel like I've had to put it out on near permanent loan."

Nigel smiled. "I'm sorry, too. I hadn't realised it was so tough. Whatever happened to that cool, calm and collected New Romantic Girl I used to know and love?"

"She's still in here somewhere - maybe she'll be able to get out again one day. I hope you still love me anyway."

"You know I do," he said quietly. I think so, anyway, he thought to himself - but I wish that once in a while you could forget being a deal maker and become a human being again.

"I love you too-whatever you may think" she replied and, to his surprise, put her arms round him and kissed him. "Come on then, Tiger" she whispered jokingly. Time for you to atone for your appalling behaviour this evening."

She pulled herself on top of him, and then gave him a teasing smile.

"Pretend I'm Jean Morton if it helps-do you wish I was?"

"No point in asking you to pretend I'm Barry-my beer gut's not big enough."

"Nor your bank balance" she laughed. "I'm sorry, I couldn't resist that."

"I like to think my personal charm and finesse make up for any inadequacy in the financial department" he smiled.

She is so gorgeous, he thought to himself-why are these moments so rare? Then he drawled, in his most seductive voice "Hey, baby, how do you fancy a really good internal rate of return?"

"Mmm. That's what every corporate financier wants" she whispered and kissed him again, before suddenly sitting bolt upright and then leaping out of bed and frantically putting some clothes back on.

"Thank goodness you said that, Nigel. I'd forgotten that I'd got to e-mail the sale and purchase agreement on Project Britney to the States tonight." Then she rushed downstairs, from where he could soon hear her laptop being switched on and the sound of fevered typing.

Great, he thought to himself. What God hath joined, no man was supposed to put asunder, but she obviously negotiated an exclusion clause for the benefit of her clients. How can conjugal rights compete with a transatlantic mega-merger?

This would never have happened with Sally, he thought-but then she is probably not even speaking to me again after tonight.

Chapter 14

Nigel spent the following day in a state of agitation over whether or not Sally had picked up his e-mail before she left for the cinema and dreading the thought that she might have been left waiting at the Tube station.

After some thought, he penned an e-mail which he hoped was suitably contrite:

To: Sally Peters
From: Nigel Troy
Hope you got my e-mail before you left for the cinema.   What a nightmare - turned out that I was invited to the opera too so had to rush off to Covent Garden. Didn't have a phone number for you. So sorry.

Spent the evening with grim client of Amanda's - Grave where is thy victory? Death where is thy sting?

Nigel

To: Nigel Troy
From: Sally Peters
No, I had obviously left before you sent your e-mail so I wound up spending 45 minutes standing around at Oxford Circus, feeling like I was auditioning for Waiting for Godot.

In the end I went and saw a film on my own - all very depressing.

This just goes to show that we shouldn't be meeting, doesn't it, Nigel? I really enjoy seeing you, but it's all wrong.

This was exactly what he had dreaded: they had been getting on so well together but this episode would inevitably have made her feel like the Other Woman-a role to which she could hardly have been less suited, either temperamentally or morally. He cursed Bodkin Manners, cursed Barry Morton and cursed Beethoven before deciding that his only chance of salvaging something was to make a play for the sympathy vote.

To: Sally Peters
From: Nigel Troy

I do know it was a disaster and that it was my fault. I can't remember when Amanda last let me loose on one of her clients - or when we last went anywhere together for that matter.

If it makes you feel better, I had a lousy time too - Amanda's client has the personal charms of Saddam Hussein and the finesse of Attila The Hun and he and Amanda talked deals all night. I felt rather sorry for his poor, downtrodden wife, who turned out to be a keen Dylan fan and really rather pleasant. Can't imagine how or why she wound-up being shackled together with him.

Nigel

She did not reply, so he decided to leave her alone for a few days, which he spent feeling very low and surprised at how emotionally involved he had become in such a short space of time. Eventually, however, he ventured a tentative overture.

To: Sally Peters
From: Nigel Troy
Hi, are you still (a) there and (b) still "speaking" to me?
I still feel awful about what happened the other night but, believe me, I did get my come-uppance.
With love
Nigel

To: Nigel Troy
From: Sally Peters
Good!

To: Sally Peters
From: Nigel Troy
I am really sorry Sally - I would have given anything to have been able to spend the evening with you.

To: Nigel Troy
From: Sally Peters
Was it really grim?

To: ***Sally Peters***
From: *Nigel Troy*
It certainly was.

To: *Nigel Troy*
From: *Sally Peters*
Like I say, good!
You deserved to suffer for standing me up!

To: ***Sally Peters***
From: *Nigel Troy*
What can I say other than how sorry I am?

To: *Nigel Troy*
From: *Sally Peters*
Well ... truth to tell, I did enjoy the film and it was one I had been wanting to see so it did not work out too badly for me - except that I did feel a bit of a saddo sitting there on my own (she said, determined to make him squirm a bit longer!)
Sally

To: ***Sally Peters***
From: *Nigel Troy*
So am I forgiven then?

To: *Nigel Troy*
From: *Sally Peters*
I suppose so!

To: ***Sally Peters***
From: *Nigel Troy*
So can we meet up again?
To: *Nigel Troy*
From: *Sally Peters*
I cannot believe I am "saying" this after all the resolutions I made last week but..term ends on Friday 25th so we could meet up one day during

the following week, if you are free....

To: Sally Peters
From: Nigel Troy
Term has ended for me now so I am pretty flexible.
Tuesday 29th??

To: Nigel Troy
From: Sally Peters
Midday?   How about Regents Park again (same meeting point as before)?   At least I can amuse myself feeding the ducks if you don't show again!!

To: Sally Peters
From: Nigel Troy
I'll be there without fail - I promise.
Nigel

To: Nigel Troy
From: Sally Peters
I believe you-thousands wouldn't....
I'm going off line now to watch the tennis.   Henman was 2 sets to love up and had broken serve in the 3ʳᵈ-so no doubt they're into the 5ᵗʰ set by now!!
Ciao
S

Chapter 15

She was waiting for him when he reached the park and smiled as he handed her a cassette tape.

"It's a piece offering, Sally, after my behaviour the other night. It's a compilation of my all-time favourite Bob Dylan tracks."

"Wow, Nigel, that's just what I always wanted. *She's Your Lover Now, Desolation Row*.... It all sounds very cheerful. What's so special about the live version of *I Threw It All* Away?"

"Apparently his estranged wife was in the audience and he belted it out with raw emotion for her benefit-it's brilliant."

"I'll look forward to listening to it when I get home: come on, let's go for a wander."

It was a glorious summer's day and they strolled around the park and then, after a light lunch at the café, sat on the grass and talked. They laughed a lot and it reminded Nigel of their day at Houghton Mill many years before.

"We are a singularly repulsive nation, aren't we?" he observed as a young couple walked past, with their bodies entwined: the boy was tall and thin with a complexion that reminded Nigel of Boo Radley from To Kill A Mockingbird, while the girl was wearing tight jeans and a crop top, from underneath which appeared several rolls of fat, a tiny naval stud occasionally glinting in the sun from among the folds of flesh.

"It all goes to prove that Darwin got it completely wrong-if those are the products of thirty thousand years of evolution, what future can there be for the human race?"

She smiled. "They look like they are blissfully in love, though, Nigel-isn't beauty in the eye of the beholder?"

"Well, the beholder should get his eyes tested" he retorted.

"I'm afraid that not every girl is able to step out with a bronzed Adonis like you-the majority of the female population have to make do with what's available. Life's so unfair, isn't it?"

"Do I detect a hint of sarcasm there, Miss Peters? It doesn't become you."

She laughed: "Sarcasm? Moi? You're getting sensitive in your old age, Nigel.

"Anyway, on the subject of Bronzed Adoni (or whatever the plural of Adonis might be) what finally became of your wife's errant assistant? Has he been returned to the bosom of the firm?"

"Well, he's been reinstated but it will be interesting to see whether his cards have been well and truly marked and whether his career will turn out to have hit the proverbial glass ceiling - that's certainly what happened after my fall from grace."

"So what was your offence? You've never said - using office furniture for immoral purposes?"

"No. I had too much to drink on a night out with Roger and then the next morning I added a dash of colour - literally - to a team meeting by being sick in a wastepaper bin. I had had a curry and by all accounts it described an elegant parabola en route from stomach to bin. The department head was singularly unimpressed, needless to say."

"I can't believe you really did that."

"It's perfectly true, I promise you. Witnesses included Robert Watson who went on to become the Grim Reaper - I can still see the almost orgasmic look of ecstasy on his face as my career prospects were consigned to the bin along with the remains of the previous night's Chicken Dupiaza."

"He sounds an awful man - is there a Mrs Reaper?"

"Apparently. She's his second wife - his first wife, Sue Huntley, had been a great friend of mine. We trained together and she used to go out with my pal, Mike, until she ditched him, quite unexpectedly, for the Reaper, which means that Mike dislikes him even more than I do. He keeps his cards close to his chest though and it wouldn't surprise me at all if he didn't instigate a palace revolution one of these days. The Reaper's safe as long as the bottom line keeps improving but once profits start to fall, I reckon he'll be toast."

"It doesn't sound like a very happy set-up."

"If you listen to Amanda, they're like the Teletubbies and all love each other very much but Mike certainly seems to have become a square peg in a round hole-he's a Cavalier and it's the Roundheads who are very much in the ascendancy…but I'm sure there are a few other closet Cavaliers there, albeit firmly confined to the closet at the moment."

"Cavaliers and Roundheads, eh?" she laughed. "Very good. Presumably you would regard yourself as a Cavalier?"

"Absolutely...and I'm sure you are too, although I suspect that you have rather more Puritanical tendencies than I do."

"There's a mix of the sacred and the profane in all of us, I'm sure, Nigel."

"I'm glad you are still speaking to me after the fiasco of our cinema trip. I do know that all this cloak-and-dagger stuff is really unsatisfactory, but I love to see you and love our e-mail chats. I hate the thought of making you feel guilty, though."

"I'm really enjoying all this too. I do feel guilty but... it's all pretty innocent isn't it, really? Why don't I give you my mobile number so that you can contact me if anything crops up another time?"

"That suggests that you're expecting there to be other times."

"Well, apart from anything else, I'm getting plenty of fresh air from these meetings, so they must be doing me some good."

"Have you got your mobile with you now? Give it here and I'll programme my number in."

Nigel watched in admiration as her fingers deftly moved on the keypad-it had taken him several days even to work out how to make and receive calls.

"Why don't you text me sometimes? It would impress the kids no end if they saw Miss Peters receiving text messages."

"My daughter managed to educate me to send e-mails and to surf the net but otherwise I'm a complete Luddite as far as any form of technology is concerned. And isn't it a generational thing? Don't you have to be under twenty to text?"

"Of course not-I'll show you." Then she sent him a quick message and showed him how to open it: *Just texting. xxx*

She gave him a crash course on composing and sending texts ("you can save time by putting '4' rather than 'for' and 'U' for 'you'") and he began to feel excited at the prospect of being able to communicate with Sally at any time of day or night.

Imagine being able to text her while she's in bed-or in the bath-he thought to himself.

When he got home that evening, he decided to test his newfound texting skills and laboriously punched out a message to her:

Missing U already. Nigel

and then selected her number from the memory on his phone and pressed "send", just before Amanda came through the front door.

"Hiya, you're home early."

"I've got a thumping headache - I was out with some investment bankers at lunchtime and I think I must have drunk too much champagne. We were celebrating that airline deal, do you remember - Project Biggles? I obviously can't take the pace like I used to. A loving husband would make me a cup of strong tea."

Matt and Galadriel were also at home and so, for what seemed like the first time in years, they sat together round the kitchen table and made a passable attempt at maintaining a conversation. We really are like the Waltons, he thought to himself as Amanda listened patiently while his daughter told them all about the recording contract that her boyfriend's band hoped to land and then his son regaled them with a blow-by-blow account of the last rugby season.

"Worst game we played was that pre-season so-called friendly against that team from up Hampstead way. A bunch of upper class thugs they were-remember? I came home with a black eye after I got a boot in the face."

"Well, you shouldn't be surprised," commented Nigel. "Didn't Napoleon or someone say that the Battle of Waterloo was won on the playing fields of Eton?"

"I think he was the one who said we were a nation of shopkeepers, wasn't he?" laughed Amanda.

"The bloke who kicked me was called Rupert Pratte-Delingpole-the lads are all looking forward to seeing him again next season."

"From a long line of aristocratic Pratts, no doubt…. That's a quote from a song called Caroline Diggeby-Pratt by Jake Thackray, if anyone's interested."

"It sounds a belter, Dad, must rush out and buy it…. You might know of this Delingpole bloke, actually, Mum-his father's a very wealthy businessman, apparently."

"It must be Sir Norman Delingpole-he's chairman of one of the big private equity houses."

She looked anxious for a moment.

"They're on our target list-you didn't thump him or anything, did you?"

"No, Mum, I just lay on the ground while he kicked me-he'll be dead meat if he plays against us next season, though, I promise you."

"Don't you dare, Matt. We've just spent a fortune taking his father to Henley and pouring champagne down the old lech's throat-I don't want you spoiling it all by putting his son in hospital."

"I'll just shake his hand and apologise for putting my face in the way of his boot, shall I then?"

"Well, if I have to put up with the father peering down my dress-all in the interests of practice development, of course, you could at least..." she began until she was interrupted by a bleep from Nigel's mobile phone which he had left on the shelf by the kitchen door, along with his car keys.

"Is that your mobile, Dad?" asked Galadriel.

"Receiving text messages, Dad?" asked Matt. "I thought that those technological advances had left you behind."

Amanda burst out laughing. "Perhaps your father's got a secret admirer. Does one of your students want to see your depreciation rates? Or fancy a bit of roll-over relief?" As she and Matt collapsed with mirth at these witticisms (Galadriel, he noticed, keeping surprisingly quiet) he was not sure which concerned him the most - the fact that he was likely to be discovered receiving what he assumed (and would in normal circumstances have fondly hoped) to be a romantic text message from Sally or the fact that his wife and son so obviously found the notion of his having an admirer completely risible.

"Aren't you going to read it, Dad?" laughed Matt, so Nigel reluctantly picked up the phone to read the message.

What a surprise to hear from you - you are so sweet. I miss you too. Not long till October though.

T xxx

Nigel's brow furrowed as he tried to make sense of the message but then he glanced at the top of the screen and saw that the name of the sender appeared as Tammy. Tammy was a secretary in his department - a prematurely middle-aged woman whom he liked to describe as Lamb

Dressed Up As Mutton. With shock, he remembered that some months previously she had programmed her mobile number into the memory of his phone for some reason that he had never been able to fathom and he realised that he had obviously sent his text message to her by mistake.

"It's from Tammy-you know, the secretary at the university. It's quite affectionate-must have been meant for her boyfriend."

I'm hopeless at dissembling, he thought to himself, aware that he had gone bright red.

"Tammy? Isn't she the one who's twenty-eight-going-on-sixty? It's hard to imagine her exchanging racy text messages with a boyfriend."

"Come on then, Dad, spill the beans: are you being pursued by a lovelorn Tammy Wynette look-alike?" asked Matt.

"She's certainly not that" retorted Nigel, rather forcibly.

"She's obviously been nursing a secret passion for you, Dad-maybe she's a real goer on the quiet."

"I'm sure she isn't" he glared.

"Is she stalking you? Do you think she's watching us from the other side of the street right now, following your every movement?"

"Perhaps I'm the one who needs to worry" guffawed Amanda. "Maybe she's going to hire a hit man to bump me off, so that she can have you all to herself."

"You want to be careful, Mum. She might follow you onto the Tube one night and then sit opposite you, giving you the evil eye while she pretends to do her knitting-then suddenly she'll leap at you and run you through with a knitting needle or gouge your eyes out with a crochet hook. It's these quiet ones who tend to be the real bunny boilers."

"Look, it was obviously a mistake, all right?" he almost shouted, becoming more and more irritated at being the butt of his wife's and his son's humour. I can't believe them, he fumed inwardly: we normally pass like ships in the night and rarely exchange more than the odd social pleasantry but now my son, in particular, is like a dog with a bone with this and will not let it drop."

"You are touchy today, aren't you? " laughed Amanda. "I think you're a little disappointed that the message wasn't meant for you."

To his relief, at that point Galadriel yawned and announced that she had to go and get ready to go out with Kieran, prompting Amanda to go off to check her e-mails and Matt to start telephoning round his friends to decide what they were going to do that evening, leaving Nigel to decide what he was going to say to Tammy.

Later that evening he e-mailed Sally to tell her what had happened.

To: Sally Peters
From: Nigel Troy
I have done a terrible thing. I texted you to say how much I was missing you but sent it to a girl I work with by mistake. She sent me a very "warm" reply, which arrived just after Amanda came home (the first time in the last 15 years that she has been home before 8.00pm except when she has been in an all night meeting).

Amanda and Matt obviously thought it a hoot to think that anybody might be sending me romantic messages, which didn't do my ego much good but what am I going to say to this girl (who rejoices under the name of Tammy)?

Hayulp!

To: Nigel Troy
From: Sally Peters
Tammy???

To: Sally Peters
From: Nigel Troy
Apparently, her father was (is) a big Country Music fan: her brothers are called Waylon and Townes (after the late Townes Van Zandt-sophisticated, huh?) and her sisters are Patsy and Loretta. According to T, he wanted to call her Dolly but her mother insisted on Tammy, on the basis that she had done more than her fair share of standing by her man.

But this is all irrelevant-what am I going to say to the woman?

To: Nigel Troy
From: Sally Peters

This is better than any soap opera! Why not just come clean and tell her it was meant for someone else, e.g. your wife?
S

To: **Sally Peters**
From: Nigel Troy
40-somethings don't text their spouses- and certainly not to tell them how much they miss them.
N

To: **Nigel Troy**
From: Sally Peters
Fair point. You could try pretending the episode didn't happen at all and hope she will have forgotten about it by next term? Otherwise, pass!
S

To: **Sally Peters**
From: Nigel Troy
You're a big help!

In the end, he sent her a suitably anodyne *Have a good summer* and decided to park that particular problem (or potential problem) until October. In the meantime, he had the prospect of the long summer vacation and hopefully plenty of opportunities to see Sally-they had arranged to meet the following Monday and he spent the next few days waiting impatiently for Monday to come.

Chapter 16

They had planned to go to see a film but the day turned out to be the hottest day of the year so far and they agreed that it would be a shame to waste it in the darkness of a cinema.

"I know, Nigel, let's be grockels for the day" was Sally's suggestion, which he readily accepted.

"How about Madame Tussauds to start with?" she proposed.

They took the Tube to Baker Street and then joined a lengthy queue, which consisted mainly of parents with young children.

"Ever since we decided to go to Baker Street, I haven't been able to get a certain Gerry Rafferty song out of my head" he remarked.

She smiled. "That record always reminds me of the Easter holidays before my A-levels. It was a lovely spring, I remember. *Baker Street* seemed to be playing everywhere."

"Great intro, but I never thought the words did justice to it.   I can remember that time, too though.   It was when it suddenly dawned on me that I'd only got one more term left at Cambridge and that after that I was going to have to face the real world."

"It comes to us all, I'm afraid."

"I know, but when I went to Cambridge the whole three years seemed to stretch ahead of me and I thought it would last forever… then suddenly it was the last term and finals were just a few weeks away."

"You and Roger invited me to your twenty first birthday party around then, didn't you? It was very sweet of you."

"I was really disappointed that you didn't come."

"I remember thinking it would be a bit awkward - I hadn't seen any of you since the previous summer, don't forget. I think as well that my parents had insisted that I go into purdah from Easter until the end of my A-levels, so I'm sure that they'd never have let me go."

"It was a good night: Saturday Night Fever had just come out and, much as I normally hate disco-type music, I rather enjoyed the film and had visions of everybody standing around and watching us dance to *More*

Than A Woman, before you fell into my arms to the strains of *How Deep is Your Love.*"

"Those things only happen in films, I'm afraid. I no doubt spent the evening with my head buried in some stimulating piece of French literature while you were out partying."

"All I can remember of it now is that things got a bit out of hand towards the end of the evening: Roger had this appalling girlfriend - Nicole, I think her name was. Anyway, she asked him to ask the disk jockey to dedicate a record to her and he asked for *Fat Bottomed Girls*. They had a blazing row and she threw a pint of Adnams all over him, which made him rant and rave at her - not because his clothes were soaking but because the barrel was running out and he was appalled at the waste. I used to think that Rog. had Adnams rather than blood in his veins - it's Beaujolais nowadays, but I guess that's middle age for you."

"The Queen's aged a bit too, since Silver Jubilee year" laughed Sally, pointing at some plastic flags bearing HM's picture.

"She certainly has - I used to think that she looked rather nubile on the old threepenny bit."

"London's a tacky place isn't it?"

"It is, but at least it's in your face - much better than those olde worlde tea shoppes of rural England, in my opinion."

"King's Parade is a bit like that now-all Cambridge college tea towels and tat like that."

"The places I hate are those National Trust houses and castles where you see a wonderful slice of history, only to emerge into the inevitable gift shop, where you are confronted with a glittering array of home-made honey and nasty little napkins and notelets, which you could buy at a tenth of the price in your local supermarket. My mother loves places like that though."

Sally laughed: "Have you been to Madame Tussauds before?"

"I must have been brought here once when I was very small because my dad has got an old black and white photo of me with Billy Wright - who was a famous Wolves and England footballer of the late fifties and early sixties, in case you didn't know. I don't think I've been since."

"We've got a photo like that at home, too - of my brother with a figure of Kevin Keegan, during his Bad Perm Years. There's also a character who looks like Mungo Jerry but who they tell me was really a goalkeeper called Peter Shilton. To think that people laugh at David Beckham's hair style!"

After Madame Tussauds, they bought a pass for an open top bus tour and then travelled up to Tower Bridge, stopping to have lunch in Covent Garden and to visit St. Paul's Cathedral, before taking a boat back to Westminster.

"I love being near water, don't you?" she sighed as they sat in a café near Westminster Pier.

"Yeah, even the grey waters of the Thames" he laughed. Have you ever heard that Bob Dylan song, *Watching The River Flow*? It's all about ennui and just chilling out - it's a brilliant song."

"You never went to Bangladesh, did you? I could have spent hours on the waterfront in Dhaka - it was really bustling and there were lots of very homespun little craft on the water - real Heath Robinson contraptions. I told you about the steam boat trip, didn't I?"

"You did-I wish Roger and I had been a bit more adventurous and done things like that."

"You'd have loved it-you might even have seen the inside of a Bangladeshi jail" she laughed. "The trip that was even better than that, though, was the boat ride through the Malabar backwaters in Kerala - it's all so green and tropical and so laid-back. You must do it one day."

"I remember that the Lonely Planet Guide listed it as one of the great journeys of India but I never got down to the south. The other one I wanted to do was the Toy Train up to Darjeeling - you needed some sort of permit, though, which involved going to the Foreigners' Registration Office in Calcutta and queuing up for hours to get the appropriate number of stamps in your passport. I couldn't quite face it in the end."

She smiled "I remember going there and it was basically just a hot and sweaty room with lots of ceiling fans whirring and lots of little men in suits wielding rubber stamps and shuffling endless pieces of paper around."

"I fear that a love of bureaucracy is one gift that the British Empire bequeathed to the Indians."

"No doubt about that: if I could secure an exclusive franchise to sell rubber stamps on the sub-continent, I would be a wealthy woman in no time at all."

"We should make a pact to go to India together one day and do the train ride to Darjeeling and your backwaters trip - maybe when we are both retired."

"You're on - as long as Amanda doesn't mind."

"I'm sure I could disappear for months on end without Amanda noticing - especially if we could time it for when she is doing one of her mega deals. We can go weeks without any form of inter-personal communication."

He leaned back in his seat and turned his face to the sun.

"The Kerala backwaters would be a far cry from the Great Ouse at Houghton Mill. I think that that was one of the most perfect days I've ever known."

She did not answer but he went on:

"I know it's a bit late to say it now, but I'm really sorry if I hurt you back then. I don't know what I was playing at."

She smiled at him. "I'm afraid that I can't say that I've been permanently scarred by the experience. You were just a youth - at that age you drift in and out of those boyfriend-girlfriend relationships, don't you?"

"I can remember you just kissing me quickly and walking out of the room. I think I'd expected you to be more upset somehow. It took a few months for me to realise that you might've been glad to see the back of me."

She shook her head.

"Histrionics have never been my style. It's a long time ago, Nigel, let's just enjoy this afternoon."

He nodded. "D'accord. I really enjoyed the Tower, didn't you?"

"It was great fun. I haven't been there since I was at school."

"I took the children once, but all Matt wanted to do was to see the chopping block. It was around the time that Andrew and Fergie separated and I think that he was expecting to see her locked up in the Bloody Tower, awaiting the executioner's axe.

"Mind you, I think that given half a chance the Royal Family would have had both Diana and Fergie executed on Tower Green years ago."

She laughed. "I'm sure you're right. Life's pretty tame nowadays isn't it?"

"Yeah, we just arrange for them to die in car accidents instead."

"You'd better be careful, Mr Cadogan-Troy, or else you'll be on your way through Traitor's Gate before you can say Camilla Parker-Bowles."

They lingered, chatting over their drinks, until Sally announced that she had to leave because she had arranged to go to a concert that night.

"With Colin?" he asked, feeling a stab of jealousy as she nodded quietly.

"Have a good time," he mumbled in an attempt to sound gracious. "Can I see you again soon?"

"How about Thursday?"

"I'm free"

"Shall we try Green Park for a change?"

"Fine by me."

"I tell you what - I'll bring a picnic. Bottom end, towards Hyde Park Corner?"

"That would be lovely-enjoy the concert...and think of me spending yet another evening with just Bob Dylan for company. Come on, I'll see you onto your train."

They headed for Westminster Tube station and stood in silence on the platform while Nigel tortured himself imagining Sally enjoying an evening of romantic music which would end with her finally succumbing to the (rather stolid, he imagined) charms of Colin.

Eventually they heard the sound of the train approaching and were pushed roughly aside by a tall, smartly dressed middle-aged man.

"He must be in a hurry for his tea" Sally smiled but then the smile froze as he suddenly stepped off the platform and into the path of the speeding train. There was a sickening thud and then a silence, which seemed to last an eternity, until it was pierced by the sound of somebody screaming.

Sally turned to Nigel and then broke down sobbing onto his shoulder as a couple of paramedics appeared - apparently from nowhere - on the platform and a disembodied (and apparently pre-recorded) voice announced that westbound services on the line were suspended until further notice owing to a fatality on the line.

He put his arm round her and steered her away, up the escalator and out into the sun.

"You need a stiff drink - come on, let's find a bar."
"A tea or a coffee will do nicely - let's go back to the café."

They returned to the café in a much more sombre mood than when they had left it: Nigel ordered a pot of tea for two and they sat and drank it without saying a word until eventually she smiled weakly at him.
"Thanks, I feel better now.... But, Nigel, it was so awful. You read about these things and expect them to be really dramatic but the way he just walked off the edge of the platform was so matter-of-fact. I can't believe how anyone could do that."
"It was pretty cold-blooded-his mind must have been well and truly made up."
"He must have been feeling absolutely desperate."
"It was a pretty selfish thing to do, though. He may have felt that he was putting his troubles behind him but what about the driver of the train? He's going to have to live with that for the rest of his life."
"It's so weird: it's a lovely summer's day up here, while down there people are having to deal with... all that. Do you think we should have stayed to give witness statements?"
"I'm sure there'll be no shortage of people giving their version of events - let's not worry."
They sat in silence again until he put his hand on hers.
"Let me see you home, Sally."
"No, honestly, I'm fine-just a little shaken still. I'll be okay but I think I'd better give the concert a miss tonight-I don't think I could sit serenely and listen to music after what's just happened."
"Let me get you a taxi then-you don't want to be going anywhere near Tube stations again today."
"That would be great, thanks, Nigel."

He decided not to e-mail her that evening for fear of bringing back memories of what had happened but the following morning he did so as soon as he was alone in the house.

To: Sally Peters
From: Nigel Troy

Morning: how are you feeling today?
N XXX

To: **Nigel Troy**
From: Sally Peters
Better thanks, Nigel.   It was awful, wasn't it?
You were lovely to me afterwards, though-thanks for that.
SX

To: **Sally Peters**
From: Nigel Troy
Kind of you to say so but I felt really helpless-I couldn't think of anything
appropriate to say.

To: **Nigel Troy**
From: Sally Peters
I was grateful to you for not saying anything-I know that sounds daft,
but it's true.   I didn't want you to try to rationalise the whole episode-I
was just glad you were with me.

To: **Sally Peters**
From: Nigel Troy
I must admit that later on I felt pretty shaken by the whole thing myself:
before it happened, the scene was so ordinary-an underground platform
packed with tourists and bored-looking commuters, nobody catching
anyone else's eye, then that happens.
I guess I've never been so close to death (someone else's!) before.
I'm sorry, this is getting a bit morbid, isn't it?   Are we still on for our
picnic?
N

To: **Nigel Troy**
From: Sally Peters
Defo!   I promise not to be maudlin-it's just that yesterday-the train,
the screams and all that-reminded me of something that happened to me
in India.

I'll tell you about it when I see you.
Sally

To: **Sally Peters**
From: Nigel Troy
Sounds intriguing....
Look forward to seeing you tomorrow.
Towards Hyde Park Corner as previously arranged?

To: **Nigel Troy**
From: Sally Peters
As the kids in my class would say, cool!
Mid-day?

To: **Sally Peters**
From: Nigel Troy
Cool.
Anything you'd like me to bring vis-à-vis the picnic?

To: **Nigel Troy**
From: Sally Peters
Just bring something to drink if you like-I think it's safest all round if I provide the food....
Any particular dislikes?

To: **Sally Peters**
From: Nigel Troy
I DETEST mayonnaise.
Otherwise not really, but am not renowned for my healthy diet....

To: **Nigel Troy**
From: Sally Peters
Chip butties all round then....
See you there.
xxx

To: Sally Peters
From: Nigel Troy
Cool!
XXX

Chapter 17

Thursday was another glorious sunny day - it was a week when the tabloid headline writers had no need to go beyond "Phew! What a scorcher" and even the broadsheets were getting excited over whether the temperature might beat the 99.8° that had been recorded in Dartford in the summer of 1976.

When Nigel arrived, Sally had spread a blanket on the ground and was unpacking a picnic hamper.

They hugged each other rather awkwardly and then sat down on the blanket.

"Can I assume that you will want to tuck into the food straightaway?" she smiled.

"Well...now you come to mention it, I do feel a little peckish. But what made you ask the question?"

"My father and I go to the Lords Test together every year and it always amuses me that he seems to feel obliged to eat his picnic as soon as we get there-I do enough food for lunch and tea but he's always scoffed the lot before play has even started. Bernadette tells me that my brother-in-law is exactly the same-it seems to be a male thing."

"Well, these sandwiches do look very good- white bread and not a dollop of mayonnaise to be seen."

"Why this pathological hated of mayonnaise?" she laughed.

"It's just one of my pet hates. In London it seems impossible to buy a sandwich that isn't dripping with the stuff. The worst thing is when they make the sandwich up in front of you and start squirting it out from a ginormous plastic bottle. It really gets my goat as does the fact that it seems de rigueur for every meal to be accompanied by a curled-up bit of lettuce and a tired-looking tomato, rejoicing under the name of a 'salad garnish'. Don't they realise that chaps like me who have steak and chips for lunch really don't want to have anything as healthy as a salad with it? It really gets my goat."

"You're so tolerant, aren't you? Do you know what I hate more than anything else? It's things that come in flat packs: how many times have I bought a nice looking cupboard or a piece of garden furniture, only to find that it comes in a flat pack, accompanied by incomprehensible diagrams or instructions that are written in German, Spanish... Greek... Serbo-Croat... every language but English?"

"I'm not convinced that flat packs can compete with mayonnaise on the goat-getting front but they do conjure up unpleasant memories of the Airfix kits that I always used to be given as a boy and which I always used to mess up. I'd wind up with the carpet covered in glue and a single-winged Concorde. One of the few good things about getting older is that nobody buys me kits any more."

He smiled. " Actually, when I think about it, I can trace the decline of my standing with my family back to Ria's third birthday when we bought her a slide which looked great in the shop but, inevitably, came in a flat-pack with the usual 'Insert Bolt R into Groove Z' and so on, accompanied by incomprehensible diagrams. The whole thing might as well have been in Serbo-Croat for all the help it was. By the time I had got it assembled, she was nine and after something a little more intellectually stimulating.

"I can still remember with shame how they looked up to me with total admiration as I began to put it together it but how that look had changed to contempt a few hours later when I was reduced to hurling abuse at the instruction leaflet and generally at the Early Learning Centre and all its works.

"Needless to say that eventually Superwoman came back from the office and did the whole thing in two minutes flat, leaving the children even more convinced that their father was a complete half-wit."

Sally laughed: " I can just imagine it. I can remember my neighbour finding me in floods of tears after a whole afternoon spent trying to put together an IKEA bookcase.

"Another thing I find really annoying" she went on "is the way that Guy Fawkes Night now seems to take up the whole of October and November."

"My goat is got rather more by the fact that as soon as the autumn term begins the Christmas decorations start going up - one year they were playing *White Christmas* in our local supermarket during August Bank Holiday week."

"On the plus side, though, once Boxing Day is over the shops start filling up with Easter eggs and I always feel that spring is on its way."

"True, but before then I have to endure the Law Faculty Christmas Dinner, which involves sitting around in silly party hats eating a shrivelled bit of turkey and some stewed sprouts, while a spotty youth sets up a disco which is our cue to make a circle and sing along to *Come On Eileen*. The only high point is watching the Dean making a complete berk of himself when he tries to dance to the *Birdie Song*."

"What a thought? We have a staff dinner and disco but thankfully the *Birdie Song* is strictly off limits. We do have a deputy head, though, who likes to strut her stuff to *Like A Virgin* - not a pretty sight. *Angel In The Centrefold* is her other favourite."

Nigel smiled at the vision that that conjured up. "At least the university Christmas bashes are safer than the Bodkin Manners Christmas parties used to be - there was a curious initiation ceremony for all young lawyers (the male ones anyway) which involved being groped (or maybe worse) by an old dragon of a secretary who rejoiced under the nickname of Halitosis Hilda. The *Conga* and the *Hokey Cokey* were the danger points in the evening."

"Were you ever one of her victims?"

"No - despite my best efforts to stand in front of her when the Conga began! Actually, I always used to put myself on a state of Red Alert once they got to *Hi Ho Silver Lining* and *Simple Simon Says* and adjourn to the bar until she'd found a victim to pounce on. Mike was less fortunate, though and I'll never hear *I'm Not In Love* without remembering the sight of him being held by her in a vice-like grip during the *big boys don't cry* bit."

"The male equivalent at my school must be a young PE teacher whom we have christened Gregory Pecs and who seems to think that every female over 30 is a frustrated *haus frau* who is desperate to feel his rippling muscles (his weapons of mass destruction, he calls them) and see his all-over sun tan. Personally, I would rather spend an evening assembling a flat pack."

He laughed: "school masters have obviously changed a bit since my day. My teachers were all middle-aged misanthropists who wore check jackets with patches on the elbows and carried with them a heady aroma of cigarette smoke, chalk dust and bad breath. The only time they would show any enthusiasm for anything was when we managed to start them on their reminiscences of doing battle with the Hun - testosterone levels in that staff room were very low, I'm sure."

I think I know now why you decided to stay so long in India - to escape IKEA bookcases and an eternal Bonfire Night."

"Maybe that had something to do with it."

She seemed so relaxed that, although he felt that he should say something about it, he delayed mentioning the episode on the Tube until after they had finished their picnic-and even then he did so with some diffidence.

"You seem to have got over the shock of...what happened the other day."

"Yes, I have, thanks. It was pretty grim, though, wasn't it?"

"In one of your e-mails you said that it brought back memories of something that happened in India: what was that all about?"

She looked down at the ground before replying.

"I had a really traumatic experience-to put it mildly-when I was there and I suppose that it was a large part of the reason why I stayed out there so long. I've only ever told my family and one or two really close friends exactly what happened but I'll tell you if you'd like me to."

"Only tell me if you want to-I don't want to pry."

It's okay. I suppose it's all part of what goes to make up Sally Peters-the 2003 version as opposed to the sweet and innocent schoolgirl you tried to seduce when you were a callow youth."

"Perish the thought."

"You were very gentlemanly and very subtle about it, I seem to remember."

"And very unsuccessful, I most certainly do remember."

"Like I said at the time, I'm not that sort of girl.... But let me tell you the story-it's pretty harrowing, I'm afraid."

Chapter 18

She had had an open invitation to visit a Professor and Mrs Singh in Delhi, who were friends of her parents - Professor Singh and her father had been at college together. He had returned to India and became a professor at Delhi University; they lived in a large house, with lovely, mature gardens, in a smart suburb of the city.

"I suspect that he came from a well-to-do family as he certainly seemed to have independent means - unless they pay their academics extremely well out there - and to be extremely well connected.

"After I'd been in Calcutta a few months, I felt in need of a break, so I got in touch with the Singhs and arranged to go and stay with them for a week or so. They looked after me extremely well and I got to see a fair bit of the city. They were a very pleasant couple, with three married daughters and a son called Raj who was a student, about nineteen or twenty, and who was obviously the apple of their eye."

One morning, she had taken a taxi into the old city and walked through the crowds along Chandi Chowk, enjoying the atmosphere in that seething mass of humanity, before making her way towards Connaught Place in New Delhi to look in the shops and then find somewhere for lunch.

"As the morning went on, I could sense that something was up - a lot of people had transistor radios to their ears and crowds were gathering round, obviously listening to some news. I assumed that something dramatic had happened in the cricket - England were over there for a test series and I had seen the excitement in Calcutta whenever a game was on.

"Eventually, I went into Nirula's restaurant for lunch and got into conversation with a girl who was clearly an Aussie or a Kiwi."

"Have you heard the news?" the girl asked, her voice shaking just a little.

"What news?"

"Mrs Gandhi has been shot - by her own bodyguards apparently.... Because of the attack on the Golden Temple at Amritsar, so I'm told. She's supposed to have been taken to hospital and there are rumours that she's dead, but there's been no official statement yet. If it's true, though, all hell's going to be let loose."

"We finished our meals and went into Connaught Place where a lot of the shops and stalls seemed to be closing. I don't know if you remember the English language bookstall there but we thought the owner might be a good person to ask for the latest news. He told us that it had been confirmed that Mrs Gandhi had been assassinated by two Sikh bodyguards."

"Go back to your hotels now and stay there - the city is not going to be safe tonight. Take a taxi and tell the driver to go fast and not to stop for anything. ... But make sure he is not a Sikh."

"There wasn't a taxi to be found, but eventually I found an autorickshaw driver who was prepared to take me back to the Singhs' for an exorbitant price - most of them seemed to be getting off the streets fast.

"It wasn't difficult to see why: as we made our way out of the city we could see smoke rising in the distance and on several occasions we saw gangs of young men armed with poles and bicycle chains marauding around the streets. At one point we saw one of these gangs beating somebody up - undoubtedly a Sikh, I later came to realise."

When she got back to the Singhs' house, Raj was already home and Professor Singh arrived about an hour later, looking grim-faced.

"They are stopping cars and buses and dragging our people out and beating them - especially the young men. And it is not just Sikhs they are attacking, but anybody who tries to help them - they came onto a bus and were hitting the passengers with sticks because they were trying to hide a Sikh family. Then they beat the whole family to death-even the children.

"The mobs are setting fire to houses and shops as well - whole neighbourhoods will be in flames soon."

Sally had listened to those accounts with a great sense of foreboding, which was increased by the urgent conversations taking place in Punjabi between Professor and Mrs Singh, punctuated by Professor Singh making various agitated - sounding telephone calls, until at last he came and sat beside her.

"You must leave Delhi now- it is not safe for you to stay here any longer. The attacks on our people are getting worse and the police are not going to do anything to stop them - worse than that, I am told that they are actually encouraging them.

"Raj will go with you - he can look after you but it is also safer for him to be out of the city. We are not so worried for ourselves - it is mainly young men who are being attacked and we should be safe.

"It is all arranged - we have a very good friend, Desai, who is a major in the Indian army. We can trust him. He is sending an army car to take you to the station and you must take a train out of Delhi - anywhere, as far as possible. You can come back when it is safe - the army must take control soon."

Not long after that, a young army officer had indeed arrived at the house in an army car, driven by a man who was evidently a military driver. Professor and Mrs Singh bundled them into a car and they set off for the station. The officer and his driver were both rather brusque and unfriendly and Sally wondered if they were unhappy to be helping a Sikh family or whether it was just that they were tense because of the situation in the city. Certainly, the atmosphere in the city was deteriorating fast: the air seemed thick with smoke as they neared the station and they passed a fair number of burnt out cars and gangs on the lookout (she assumed) for more Sikh victims.

The station was surrounded by soldiers but they saluted and allowed the car through, whereupon the young officer told them to follow him and then led them into an office.

"Wait here until I come back" he told them curtly and then disappeared.

"Can we trust him?" she asked Raj.

"We have no choice. There will be many people waiting to leave Delhi and there will be no other way to get a ticket."

They stood together in silence until he returned.

"Come with me please" he barked and led them through a large crowd of people to an empty carriage.

"This train goes to Jaipur and then onto Ajmer. Get in please."

"Will it be safe for us in Jaipur?" she asked.

"I do not know: you will have to see when the train arrives there. I think that Ajmer may be safe."

"The train seemed to be absolutely packed and I had no doubt he had used his position - and maybe a little bribery - to make sure we had a carriage to ourselves. I'm afraid that by then I was just thankful to be able to get away."

"We are so grateful - thank you so much" she tried to smile at the officer but he simply nodded and turned away.

The first hour or so was quiet and uneventful but then she felt the train come screeching to a halt, apparently in the middle of nowhere, and instinctively she knew that this was a bad sign.

"There was a lot of shouting and opening and slamming doors and then the screams began - we guessed what was happening: Sikh passengers were being attacked by a mob.

"Then our door was flung open and a couple of red-eyed thugs with knives and bicycle chains climbed in. They looked at Raj and then at me and began to talk quickly in Hindi, looking at me all the time. One of them called me a whore and-I wouldn't like to tell you what else- and pushed me down. He held me there while the other one began to open up his *dhoti* - I knew he was going to rape me. All I can remember about him was that he had protruding teeth, stained with betel juice, and smelled of stale sweat.

"They seemed to have forgotten about Raj until he suddenly leaped up and made a dash for the door. I'm sure that he just wanted to get them to leave me alone and it worked - I could hear shouting from further up the train and then the men who were with me left me and jumped out after Raj. I heard someone shouting, then a scream - which I knew was Raj's - and then silence.

"I didn't stop to find out what had happened - I jumped out of the door and ran like crazy. I heard some shouts and thought I heard someone following me, but I had left my backpack on the train and was wearing trainers, so I could run pretty fast. I suppose that we were really only a few miles beyond the outskirts of Delhi, but it was all very rural and I hardly saw a soul.

"I don't know how long I ran for, but I was desperate to put as much distance as possible between myself and the mob on the train. When I couldn't run any more, I found a small clump of trees and went in there for a sleep. Being October, it got quite cold, but I slept like a baby for a few hours, then I woke up just before dawn, feeling desperately tired and hungry. I couldn't even begin to get my mind around what had happened the night before.

"It's a long story, but eventually I found a village where the head man - or whatever he would be called - spoke some English and I was able to explain that I had left Delhi, because there was trouble there and that my train had been attacked. For obvious reasons, I didn't mention Raj. Fortunately, I had plenty of money in a money belt and managed to get them to agree to let me stay there for a few days and to keep me fed and watered.

"The family I stayed with were very kind and left me to my own devices most of the time - the reality of what had happened was beginning to sink in and I thought a lot about Raj and his parents and about when and how I was going to get back to Delhi.

"After 3 or 4 days, a couple of the men from the village ushered me into a hut, making cutting gestures with their fingers on the way. It turned out that the man whose hut it was had a transistor radio and I guessed that the snipping charade was their way of telling me that he had a radio because he had taken advantage of Sanjay Gandhi's radio-for-a-vasectomy initiative. It was the first smile I had had for days.

"Anyhow, from the radio I managed to establish that there had been terrible violence in Delhi but that the army had belatedly restored order. A couple of days later I was back in Delhi, after a journey involving ox-cart, bus and train."

She took a taxi to the Singhs' house and Professor Singh opened the door.

"Sally, it is good to see that you are safe."

"How are you, Professor Singh?"

"It has been terrible in Delhi: the army restored order eventually but in their own time. Many of our friends have had their houses burned and some of them have been attacked. But this area is mainly Hindu, so we have been safe."

He waved his hands dismissively.

"But that is not so important. Tell us what has happened to you - and where is Raj?"

She hesitated "Have you heard any news at all of Raj?"

"No. Desai told us that his men had put you on a train for Jaipur but no more."

With a sick feeling in her stomach, Sally told them the story of the attack on the train and how Raj had saved her but had then been attacked himself.

"He must have been very badly beaten... They were murderous thugs.... I'm afraid that he may have been killed."

"It was the worst moment of my life, Nige" - they seemed to age years before my eyes and I would have given anything in the world to have been able to have given them some hope - but that mob was hell-bent on murder.

"I was able to give them a reasonably good indication of where the attack happened and Professor Singh got onto the phone to this Desai who came round to the house a couple of days later to say that his people had found a heap of half-burned bodies by the railway line and that they thought that one of them was Raj. I don't know how they could tell but Professor Singh went somewhere and identified him.

"It was too awful for words - they were absolutely devastated as you can imagine.

"I stayed for the funeral, then I headed back to Calcutta - I felt I'd brought them enough trouble. I've never seen them since, but we've kept in touch by letter.

"This may sound corny, but I felt that their son had given his life to save mine and that I owed it to them to stay in Calcutta and give something back to the country. I am sure that if Raj had just stayed at home, he would have been fine. I would've been fine there too, but they were so desperate to make sure that I was safe."

As she reached the end of her story, Nigel felt a sudden surge of affection for her and a deep sadness that she had had to endure such traumas, just a few years after those golden days in Cambridge.

He took her hand and squeezed it - and then looked up to see Amanda and a couple of middle-aged men in suits heading across the park, directly towards them.

Chapter 19

Dropping Sally's hand like the proverbial hot potato, Nigel did a very passable (if totally unintentional) impersonation of Lance Corporal Jones from Dad's Army. He did not actually say "don't panic!" but the message was written all over his face.

After looking frantically around for a hiding place, he hurled the remains of their picnic onto the floor and threw the blanket over his head; that was how he stood until Sally informed him that Amanda had gone past.

"Do you think she saw me?" he asked, once the blanket had been removed and he had emerged, rather shame-facedly, into the sunlight.

"I'm sure she didn't. Frankly, Nigel, they all seemed to be engrossed in their conversation - presumably some exciting new deal - and I think you could have hopped around on one leg completely naked singing *Land of Hope And Glory* without them noticing you."

Nigel said nothing, feeling extremely embarrassed. Sally, however, suddenly dissolved into fits of helpless laughter.

"Oh, Nigel, you are a complete basket case but I do love you. You looked like one of those ghosts and ghoulies out of Scooby Doo. Any moment I expected Shaggy or Velma to rip the blanket off you and for you to say 'fair cop - pesky kids' or whatever they always said when they were nicked."

Nigel began to laugh too, until the import of Sally's words began to sink in.

He reached out and put his arms round her. "I love you too" he said quietly and then kissed her. He rather expected her to draw away, but she returned his kiss and they stood kissing for some time, until she bent down to spread out the blanket again, then sat down and drew him down with her.

He lay back, she put her head on his lap and then they stayed there in silence for some minutes, savouring the moment.

Eventually he asked her: "It's a long time since my ego has been massaged, so what do you find so loveable about me?"

She laughed mischievously: "Your sublime good nature of course."

She paused, and then went on.

"You're quite a flawed character, really, and I love that - you're very bright but nobody could ever describe you as driven and you seem to be destined to spend the rest of your three-score-years-and-ten firmly cocooned in the nineteen seventies."

"What makes you think that?"

"Well, the eighties and nineties seem to have by-passed you completely - so the twenty-first century is unlikely to stand a chance of permeating into your world.

"But you make me laugh like nobody else has ever done…and you're kind and considerate in a rather distracted sort of way."

"I guess I'll take that as a compliment."

"It was meant to be, I promise."

"I can't believe how happy you make me feel, Sally - I love every second I spend in your company. It was as though I was living like half a man before we met up again."

She convulsed with laughter again.

"Living like half a man! That's straight from a Beach Boys' Song - *Darlin'* wasn't it? You'll be telling me next that I'm giving you the excitations."

"So where do we go from here?" he asked eventually.

"I don't know - and I can't bring myself to think about that right now. All I know is that I'm really happy so let's just take it one day at a time and, if nothing else, let's give each other some memories."

Over the next couple of weeks, they met most days. The weather continued to be hot and sunny, so they generally met in a park but one day, to his delight, she agreed to come with him to the Oval where Surrey were playing Worcestershire, the county which he still supported.

The only weekday they did not meet was the day when she told him that she had arranged to go to Stratford.

"With Colin, by any chance?"

"Yes, I am going with Colin. We fixed this up weeks ago and I can't back out now."

He was silent for a bit, feeling irrationally jealous and angry that he was not free to do things like that with her.

"It's strange, Sally" he said at last. "When you say you're doing something with Colin, I do hope you have a nice time - but I also dread that you will."

She smiled at him-rather sadly, he thought. "How do you think I feel when we part and I know that you are going back to Amanda? I know you say that you lead separate lives but she's still the one you go home to-and, if you'll forgive me for lowering the tone, the one you snuggle up to at night."

He hesitated for a few moments. "A propos of which, Sally, there is one thing I wanted to mention to you. Please don't be cross with me for saying this but on Thursday and Friday I'm lecturing to a bunch of solicitors and accountants at a hotel near Richmond and the people who have organised the conference are putting me up for the night there.

"I was wondering if you would like to come to the hotel so that we could spend some more time together."

He flushed and then went on: "If you'd like to stay over with me on the Thursday night that would be wonderful but otherwise I'd just love to see you."

She looked down at the ground: "I don't know, Nigel. Don't get me wrong - I love spending every possible moment with you - but I'm not sure that assignations with married men in seedy hotel rooms are really 'me' - it seems so sordid, somehow."

She was quiet for a few moments, then said quietly: "It would be lovely, though, I do know that - I don't know what to say."

He took her hand. "I know how you feel but... I guess I just take the view that this life isn't a rehearsal and that you need to take your opportunities to find happiness wherever you can."

"Yes, but not at somebody else's expense - I'm thinking about your wife and family."

"Look, Sally, you don't need to decide now: I'm going to be staying there anyway and I'll e-mail you the details. There's a drinks reception and a buffet meal after the close of play on the Thursday night and after that I'll go back to my room. If you'd like to come, you'll find me there any time from about eight o'clock - no need to phone or text, just turn

166

up. I'd love it if you did but if not… well, hey, there's still a couple more weeks left of the second Summer of Love."

She smiled. "Okay, we'll leave it that I'll see you if I see you. Thanks for being so sweet."

Chapter 20

The prospect of spending two hot summers' days lecturing to a motley collection of solicitors and accountants at a conference with the punchy title of "Tax Update for Professionals - With Particular Emphasis On the New Regime for the Taxation of Employee Shares" would normally have filled him with gloom. The prospect of a long evening-and possibly even the whole night-with Sally, however, made the rather non-descript hotel on the A316 near Richmond feel to him like Nirvana.

He was required to deliver two hour-long sessions - one, on the Thursday afternoon on "Obtaining Relief from Income Tax and Sheltering Capital Gains under the Enterprise Investment Scheme" and the other, the following morning on "Employee Share Schemes after the Finance Act 2003" and on the Thursday he had to struggle hard to keep his mind on the riveting subject-matter of his contribution rather than on what might or might not happen in his hotel room that evening.

The delegates at the conference basically divided into two distinct groups - the keen ones who clearly paid attention to his every word and took extensive notes throughout and those who were obviously there because their firms had told them to go or because they were in urgent need of Continuing Professional Development points.

At the close of proceedings for the day, he was morally obliged to mingle with the attendees over drinks and over the rather tired-looking buffet supper that followed but somehow he managed to survive that ordeal without making it too obvious that he was mentally somewhere else - in his room, tasting the thrill of stolen love (who wrote those words-was it Gram Parsons? he wondered) with Sally, to be more precise.

He finally made his excuses at about half past seven and had a quick shower and change of clothes before eight o'clock, which was the time when he had told Sally that he should be free.

The days of Brut anti-perspirant and swallowing toothpaste were long gone, as were the flared jeans and cowboy boots -instead, his pulling gear

2003-style comprised a pair of lightweight summer trousers (blue) and a red polo shirt.

It was only when he had showered and changed and was sitting quietly in the subdued light of the lava lamp that added a touch of seventies tackiness to the room that he was able to bring himself to think about what the evening (and night) ahead might have in store. It was quite conceivable that she would not show up at all, but he did not allow himself to dwell on that possibility. If she did come, would she stay the night? If so, what would happen? All he really hoped for was that she would come - he would be perfectly content just being with her for as long as possible.

He sat there in a state of nervous anticipation, thinking that every set of footsteps in the corridor outside must be Sally arriving and feeling deflated every time they passed by his door.

To pass the time, he began (mentally) to compile a Post-Cambridge Seduction Tape 2003 style, which was not easy as he had ceased to take an interest in what was happening in the music world in the early nineteen eighties - by Live Aid, at the very latest.

Nothing Compares 2 U by Sinead O'Connor and *Holding Back The Years* by Simply Red were the only records that he could remember from the intervening years, so he allowed himself to stretch back into the more distant past to include *Stay With Me Till Dawn* by Judy Tzuke and *Will You?* by Hazel O'Connor.

When he tired of that, he paced round his room and began to prepare a mental inventory of its contents which, he thought, were exactly the same as the contents of every other hotel room in which he had stayed during the last twenty years - the clothes cupboard with its sliding doors and thief-proof coat hangers, along with the trouser press and small safe; the mini bar from which he could buy drinks and chocolate at extortionate prices; the miniature electric kettle accompanied by a few tea bags, small plastic containers of UHT milk and some sachets of sweetener; the bathroom with the bottles of shampoo and body lotion, the neatly-wrapped tablets of soap and the complimentary sewing kit.

It was all rather depressing, he concluded: if you were taken at random to any hotel anywhere in the western world, this was what you would find - just as, if you were parachuted into the high street of any decent-sized town in England, you would find it almost impossible to work out where you were, as everywhere you would find the same pedestrianized precincts, with the same shops (Boots, Dixons, Body Shop, Laura Ashley), the same places to eat (MacDonalds, Pizza Hut) and the same themed pubs and bars, with identical menus. For a moment, he even began to lament the passing of Berni Inns and the prawn cocktails and Arctic Rolls of yesteryear.

After that, he tried to amuse himself by thinking of a rock band beginning with every letter of the alphabet but it only took a couple of minutes to go from Argent to ZZ Top, so he began to compile a mental list of songs about hotels that did not include the obvious *Hotel California* and *Heartbreak Hotel*, leaving him with *Memory Motel* by the Rolling Stones (which seemed singularly inappropriate to his present circumstances as a lonely room was not exactly the stuff of which memories are made) and Loudon Wainwright III's *Motel Blues*.

Then he moved on to rock stars with the same names as footballers but could only come up with Allan Clarke (Leeds United and the Hollies) and Neil Young (Manchester City and Crosby, Stills, Nash and Young) and began pacing the room again.

This, he decided, was another evening to add to the Nigel Troy List of Great Romantic Disappointments - along with the Love Triangle (as the tabloids would call it) with Amanda and Tarquin, the evening with Debbie Such and, of course, the last night in Dinard. There was also, a half-remembered episode involving a cross-eyed medical student (Charlene?) he had met on a cable car in San Francisco and a disastrous evening at a youth club disco where a girl he had long fancied took an immediate and inexplicable fancy to Rick Powis.

He had gone home in disgust that evening and paced round his bedroom in the way that he was doing now, before writing in his diary "Perfidia! I shall never smile again."

Mercifully, the following day Wolves had beaten Manchester City in the League Cup final and he had forgotten all about her until now. In the hope that history might repeat itself, he put on the Test Match highlights but even the still relatively novel experience of watching England win a game failed to lift his spirits, as did the sudden realisation that in those days Fulham had a winger called Steve Earle, which gave a third name on his lift of footballers who shared their name with rock stars.

Eventually, unable to bear it any longer, he telephoned her home number but there was no reply (and he went to bed,) feeling exceedingly flat and dischuffed with life until he was brought up short by the sudden realisation that, once again, he had failed to give a moment's thought to Amanda and his children. He was what the tabloids would call a Love Rat, albeit one who was having to spend a lonely night in a third rate hotel-a far cry from the Love Nests where the subjects of the tabloid headlines apparently spent their nights of passion.

Despite these pangs of guilt, the first thing he did on his return home the next afternoon was to e-mail her:

To: **Sally Peters**
From: **Nigel Troy**
Sorry not to have seen you last night - it would have been wonderful.
Called you at home but no reply, so guessed you must have had a better offer! Colin, I presume?
N
To: **Nigel Troy**

From: **Sally Peters**
Nigel, I did come to the hotel at about 8 o'clock but reception told me that there was no Nigel Troy staying there.
I sat around in the bar for an hour or so on the off chance that you would come looking for me, but there was no sign of you.
What happened? Did you stay somewhere else?

To: **Sally Peters**
From: **Nigel Troy**
No, I was staying in room 327. I don't understand this.

It was only after he had sent this e-mail that the likely truth dawned.

To: Sally Peters
From: Nigel Troy
xxxx! I was booked in as Nigel Cadogan-Troy!
Blast Amanda and her xxxxxxxxx pretensions!
Nigel

To: Nigel Troy
From: Sally Peters
*Oh, no, I am sure you are right. I certainly asked for Nigel **Troy** - I had forgotten all about your hyphen.*
I seem to make a speciality of being stood up by you for one reason or another, don't I? Oxford Circus, hotels in Richmond....
It was awful, actually, Nigel. I sat in the bar minding my own business and got chatted up by a really sleazy, lounge lizard sort of chap. A used-car salesman, I am sure.
He obviously thought I was on the game and when I said I was a teacher he got really excited and said he was a naughty boy and needed firm discipline....
In the end I went out on the pretext of powdering my nose and then legged it to the car and drove off like Michael Schumacher.
S

To: Sally Peters
From: Nigel Troy
I'm sorry Sal - and so disappointed. I was really excited all Thursday at the thought of spending the evening (or more...) with you and spent today feeling like a child who had been told that Christmas has been cancelled.
Can I see you on Monday?
Nigel

To: Nigel Troy
From: Sally Peters
I am off to Cambridge on Sunday to stay with my parents - remember?
I have an idea, though. Why don't you come to Cambridge one day

*and we can revisit some old haunts - maybe have lunch at the Spade &
Becket, a drink at the Alma Brewery...?*
    S

To: Sally Peters
From: Nigel Troy
That would be heavenly.
How about Tuesday?
*I've checked train times from Liverpool Street and there's one that gets
into Cambridge at about 11 o'clock - I could get that one.*

To: Nigel Troy
From: Sally Peters
*That would be fine - I'll have my car, so I'll collect you at the station
and we can head into town and have some fun....*
    S

To: Sally Peters
From: Nigel Troy
How about lunch at the Golden Egg for old times' sake?

To: Nigel Troy
From: Sally Peters
*I don't know how to tell you this, Nigel, but...that particular
establishment disappeared years ago (as did the Athena poster shop next
door, by the way).   It is one of life's delicious ironies that the Golden
Egg-purveyor of gunky sausage, beans and chips for much of the 1970s-
is now a health food shop.*

To: Sally Peters
From: Nigel Troy
*Whaaat? Is nothing sacred? You will be telling me next that the Whim
has now been taken over by the Body Shop....*

To: Nigel Troy

From: Sally Peters
Laura Ashley actually-or maybe it's Liberty's. It hasn't been a restaurant for about 20 years....

To: Sally Peters
From: Nigel Troy
Philistines! No night out was complete without a trip to the Whim to line the stomach with their Moussaka And Grease special.
*Your mention of Athena brings back some memories too- that was where I bought **the** poster, the one of the girl in the tennis skirt and no knickers. Remember?*

To: Nigel Troy
From: Sally Peters
How could I forget it hanging on your wall, next to a tasteful picture of somebody apparently flushing himself down the loo, if my memory serves me well....

To: Sally Peters
From: Nigel Troy
Just think, the girl in the photo is probably a grandmother by now.
I like to think that she might be a female Dorian Gray, with the face of an 18-year old, while her backside ages on thousands of Athena posters.

To: Nigel Troy
From: Sally Peters
Yeuch!
TTFN-see you in Cambridge!
Sally xx

To: Sally Peters
From Nigel Troy
I can't wait: see you then.
Nigel
xxx

To: **Nigel Troy**
From: **Sally Peters**
xxxxxx

Chapter 21

So effervescent was Nigel's mood as the train pulled out of Liverpool Street Station, that he resolved there and then that he would not allow himself to be annoyed by the man sitting opposite him, who had begun talking into his mobile phone at full volume the moment he sat down.

"Hello, Jennifer? Trevor here. I'm on the train.

"Jennifer, I've seen the letter from Margaret's solicitor and you need to get back to him straightaway - it's complete fabrication. Nothing happened that night she was staying at her mother's - I was at the Lodge until two o'clock in the morning... You know, the Masonic Lodge."

As Trevor continued with his denials of infidelity, Nigel began to recall the excitement of going back to Cambridge for a new term.

After an hour or so of boring motorway driving, they would grind slowly through Northampton and Bedford and then through St. Neots. His excitement would begin to mount as they passed the American Military Cemetery at Madingley but his favourite moment was when they turned off the Bedford road towards the city centre and he would begin to look out for familiar faces.

How he wished that he was on his way back now for another year in Bateman Street, with Pete and Roger in the same house and Sally just a ten minute bicycle ride away.

These thoughts were rudely interrupted by Trevor, who was now yelling down the phone at (he assumed) his accountant.

"Bob? It's Trevor. I'm on the train... ON THE TRAIN.

"Look, I've agreed a deal with the other side. They'll pay me some more money if next year's profits - before tax - are more than eight hundred thousand. The deal is three times the profit over eight hundred grand, up to a maximum of four hundred and fifty grand. Got that?

"Can you brief the lawyers then? Thanks, Bob, speak to you later."

While the journey to Cambridge had always been exciting, as silence fell, Nigel began to recall how low he would often feel on his return to the Midlands at the end of term. His depression would normally begin as they approached the Fort Dunlop factory alongside the M6-it all seemed so different from the cloistered world of Cambridge and its ancient university.

Almost immediately, however, Trevor began to embark on another conversation with (presumably) his secretary.

"Sheila? I'm on the train. Could you do me a favour please, love?

"Can you make me an appointment to see Dr Hennin tomorrow - any time - about these haemorrhoids?

"What? I said HAEMORRHOIDS. He'll know what they are. Hello, Sheila? SHEILA?"

By the time these instructions had been safely communicated to the faithful Sheila, the train was already dawdling into Cambridge station and it was not long before Nigel saw the figure of Sally waiting on the platform for him.

Rising from his seat, he smiled cheerfully at Trevor.

"I hope you don't mind my saying this, but the tax structure of your deal is all wrong. You may find that you're taxed on the value of your earn-out whether or not you actually receive anything.... And make sure that you get some security for the payment."

Ignoring his companion's surprised look, Nigel fixed him with another beatific smile.

"I hope you sort out your local difficulties with your wife - these things can happen to the best of us, nothing to be ashamed of - and that your little health problems clears up.... You know," he whispered confidentially "the old Farmer Giles."

On that happy note, he sauntered off to find Sally, whistling *Itchycoo Park* as he went.

After a long embrace, she took him by the hand and led him to her car.

"You're coming on a magical mystery tour with me, my lad" she announced. "And you can take that lecherous grin off your face - it's going to be a highly respectable day out."

She opened the glove compartment and held up an aged-looking cassette case. "Here's your first treat of the day-just to prove that you aren't the only romantic one. I got hold of a copy after we split up because it reminded me of you."

She put the tape into the cassette player and he heard Dave Lambert's familiar guitar riff from the beginning of *Angel Wine*. "Impressed, huh?"

"I'm really touched, Sally" he laughed. "Can I play air guitar as we travel?"

They headed down Station Road and then along Bateman Street for a nostalgic look at the house where he used to live (now converted into luxury apartments) before making towards the city centre and then driving along the Backs.

To Nigel's surprise, instead of stopping by the river, they carried on towards Huntingdon and began to leave the city behind.

"Where are you taking me? I assumed we were going to do the usual tourist bits and maybe have a romantic trip on the river - I'm sure I haven't lost my legendary technique with a punt pole."

"I've got something far more poignant lined up for you" she smiled as they joined the busy highway that the Huntingdon Road had become since his day.

It was only when she turned off through Fenstanton and he saw the sign for the villages of Houghton and Wyton that he realised that they were going back to Houghton Mill, the scene of that idyllic April day back in the summer of 1977.

By the time they reached the mill, the early mist had cleared and it was another glorious summer's day; they stood by the lock and watched the boats for a time and then strolled hand in hand across the meadow.

"I love the openness of East Anglia and its big skies- I know it lacks rolling hills and dramatic landscapes, but there's something special about it, all the same. From my window in Ealing I mostly see other houses and the odd rather sad-looking pollarded tree, with just a tiny patch of sky here and there."

"I fear I'm a dyed-in-the-wool townie" he laughed " but I must admit, London's a pretty grim place to be on a day like this."

"Just think how different life might have been if you'd read classics rather than law at Cambridge. You might have wound up as a don and become the world's leading expert in the use of the Iota Subscript in Homeric Poetry or something equally arcane."

"I often wish I'd done just that. I'd have worn an old sports jacket and ridden round on a bike with all my worldly goods in a basket on the front. I think that a life of genteel poverty would have suited me-mind you, as it is, it's just my wife's earnings that keep me from having to sell the Big Issue in my spare time, so I'm half way there. I've got the poverty but lack the gentility."

After lunch at a pub in Hemingford Abbots (where 1977's Scampi-In-The-Basket had been replaced by various Thai and Vietnamese dishes) they walked back to Houghton Mill and hired a punt. Drifting quietly along the backwaters of the Great Ouse, Nigel began to serenade her with a favourite Strawbs' song about late summer falling asleep, which seemed to sum up the afternoon perfectly.

Afterwards they stretched out in the grass by the river and talked and kissed, as they had done twenty-six years previously.

"So" she asked eventually, " is this how you remember the place?"

"Pretty much, although it seems greener and more lush somehow-but then it was much earlier in the year when we came before, wasn't it?"

He sat thoughtfully for a few moments.

"Do you know that poem by Thomas Hardy, where he goes back to a place he and his wife had visited in their youth and which had obviously stayed in his memory for the rest of his life? *Old love's domain* was how he described it."

"I know the poem you mean At Castle Boterel, it's called."

"It can be a bit disorientating sometimes when you go back somewhere - everything seems to be the same, but not quite the same, if you know what I mean."

"I found it really weird going back to India after a dozen years or so-it was a place I'd known really well and the changes were quite subtle but still rather disconcerting."

"Why was that?"

"The faded grandeur of Delhi and Calcutta was there-maybe a little more faded, if anything-but it seemed a lot less foreign somehow. In the cities, they all seemed to be chattering into their mobile phones and my hotel room in Delhi had satellite TV-there is something unreal about being in India and watching Blind Date."

He grimaced at the thought.

"It was much more fun when you had to be content with dubbed versions of British TV programmes-we watched Are You Being Served in Italian in a hotel in Ravenna   and it was a hoot-Roger speaks fluent Italian and could tell that all the references to Mrs. Slocombe's, er, feline friend were completely lost on the natives.   I'm not sure how Cilla having 'a lorra, lorra laffs' would dub into Hindi though."

They sat quietly and watched a boat pass through the lock before she turned to him, rather sadly.

"I'd love to meet Pete and Roger again.   I'd ask you to pass on my regards but I suppose that would be inappropriate in the circumstances. It's quite strange being with you without them being around - they seemed to be an ever-present part of our relationship."

"We've grown apart a little over the years but they're still the best friends I'll ever have."

"Do the three of you still compile endless lists when you meet?   I always remember sitting quietly while you put together your All-Time Top Ten Songs, All-Time Top Albums, Ten All-Time Favourite Films and so on."

"Were we really such a bunch of anoraks?" he laughed.

"You were quite - it was very entertaining, though, at times.   Come on, then, what would be your Desert Island Discs 2003 selection?"

"Well, I'd certainly have to have something by Strawbs and I think I'd take *Angel Wine*, because it would remind me of today, as well as Cambridge."

He wrinkled up his nose before continuing.

"I'd want some Dylan - probably something off *Desire* as I think it reminds me of Cambridge more than anything else does.   I'd also want *Honky Tonk Women* to remind me of teenage discos and to give me something to bop around to if the mood took me...and something by Led Zeppelin to remind me of those far-off days in the sixth form common room at school - *Stairway To Heaven* would be too obvious, so I think it would be *When The Levee Breaks*."

"I pity Man Friday if he encounters you strutting your funky stuff to the Stones or playing air guitar to Led Zep. He might need breaking in gently-some Petula Clark or Rolf Harris perhaps."

"I don't fancy being marooned on a tropical island with only *Two Little Boys* or *Jake The Peg* to listen to, thank you very much."

"I don't know about that: they'd make me realise that life on a desert island wasn't so bad after all."

"Good thinking, Batman. On that basis, perhaps I should take *Agadoo* as well. Then I'd never worry about trying to escape. I'd rather take *December '63* by the Four Seasons though-that always reminds me of meeting you for the first time."

"Except that we met in 1977...and it was February or March."

"February, actually, but you're being pedantic-it's a lovely innocent song about meeting somebody special for the first time."

"I like that one too-it reminds me of the first year sixth at school. That was a fun year."

"I'd want something else to remind me of you-probably *I Will* off the Beatles' *White Album*. I know that it's one of those slushy Paul McCartney numbers that I used to profess to dislike but it sums up how I feel about you and finding you again."

He was quiet for a couple of minutes. "This is going to destroy my street cred. completely but I've half a mind to go for *Barbados* by Typically Tropical for my last selection. It was at the top of the charts around the time my A-Level results came out and it suddenly began to sink in that I really was off to Cambridge in just a few weeks time. Can you remember the summer of seventy five?"

"Not specifically, Nigel, no" she laughed.

"It was a glorious summer and England were playing Australia- there was a grey-haired batsman called David Steele who seemed to be defying the Australians almost single-handedly. John Arlott's Wessex burr seemed to be everywhere and somehow it seemed as though my childhood was ebbing away very slowly and pleasantly. I remember the excitement-and the apprehension too as I knew that it would all be very different from Dudley."

"A psychologist would have a field day with your choice of music, Nigel I'm sure you'd be marked down as a man who's living in the past."

He thought for a moment. "Actually, on second thoughts, I think that I'd leave *Barbados* behind and take *The Wing And The Wheel* by Nanci Griffith. Have you ever heard of her? She's a Texan so-called New Country, singer-she's about our age and tends to sing about…well, being our age."

"I can't say I have - country music wasn't exactly big in Calcutta."

"She's brilliant - that song always reminds me of my Cambridge friends. The last verse goes:

Here's to all the dreamers
May our open hearts find rest
(Something, something)
We'll have memories for company
Long after every song's been sung."

Sally laughed: "It sounds like a song that sums you up perfectly-you're still an incorrigible dreamer, aren't you? And I still think that you're living on your memories-even *Angel Wine* must be thirty years old. Let's move on to your book though, before you start changing your mind again. What would you choose?"

"Could I take *Cannery Row* and *Sweet Thursday by John Steinbeck*? They're both very short and I couldn't choose between them."

"I suppose I could allow that - my choice would be *A Suitable Boy* and I suspect that that would be about five times as long as your two books combined. What would be your luxury item?"

"An endless supply of Wagon Wheels, I think. What would be yours?"

"Tom Cruise, ideally… only joking, Nigel, of course I'd want to have you with me, even if I couldn't compete with Wagon Wheels for your affections. Years ago, by the way, I thought that Linda Ronstadt and Emmylou Harris were the competition."

"My dad always maintained that he came a poor second to Englebert Humperdinck in my mother's affections-little did he know that in later years she would have to play second fiddle to organic compost in his.

Anyhow, what would be your choice of music?"

"I'm not so sure-I sense that you've already given the matter plenty of thought, but I've never really bothered. My tastes are pretty catholic (as you'd expect from a Papist like me, I know). I'll have to give it some thought but I would certainly choose a Beethoven symphony (not sure which one), an operatic aria or two and some Indian music... and also *Horse With No Name,* as that reminds me of going camel trekking into the Thar desert from Jaisalmer."

"Why does a song about a horse remind you of camel trekking?"

"It's all about the desert, isn't it? That's near enough for me. I'd have to have something to remind me of you too - probably *Angel Wine.*"

"Not *Making Plans For Nigel?*"

"I'd forgotten that one-probably with good reason. I'd want something a bit more upbeat, like *Walking Back To Happiness*-Helen Shapiro, was it? I think that's about the most cheerful song I know so it would lift me up whenever I felt down."

"The song that's playing in my head at the moment is relatively up to date - do you know *Days Like This* by Van Morrison?"

"No: I was never really into Van The Man. He always seems a grumpy old goat to me."

"He's not exactly a little ray of sunshine but he's pretty talented, all the same. Anyway, *Days Like This* is a song about those days when everything just seems to fall into place and all is right with the world. I guess that's how I'm feeling right now."

She did not answer, so he went on.

"I'll never forget this one Sunday in Cambridge: it had snowed over night and on the Sunday we had lunch at the Eagle and then went for a walk along the backs; after that we went back to Pete's room and had brandy butter on toast. I remember kneeling down and using a bent coat hanger to toast the bread on his gas fire and then he put on Radio Caroline and *Native New Yorker* was playing. The song wasn't really my scene and there was nothing particularly special about the moment but I suddenly felt completely happy and content-like God was in his heaven and all was well with the world. Whenever I hear that song-and often when I smell toast-I remember the feeling."

"I know what you mean. C.S. Lewis called it being surprised by joy.

It was the title of his autobiography, in fact."

"Why?"

"His theory was that those moments are a reflection of what heaven would be like - it's rather a nice thought."

"It would be heavenly if we could always be together."

"We can't though, Nigel, can we?"

"All the more reason to treasure days like this" he said quietly.

"I liked the words of that last song you mentioned - the one about the dreamers. How did it end again?"

"We'll have memories for company long after every song's been sung."

"That says it all, doesn't it, really?"

She sat quietly for a time, then went on: "The trouble is that I'm not sure that dreams are enough for me-you can't live out your life in your memory, can you?"

They lapsed into a long silence and Nigel suddenly felt overwhelmed by a delicious melancholy at the thought that at the end of the day they would have to go their separate ways and that it was likely to be a long time before they would be able to spend another summer's day together, if they ever did.

"A lot's happened since we were last here together" he sighed eventually, in a bid to break the silence.

"It certainly has-it's terrifying."

"We ain't that young any more but…. did you ever hear the new lines Paul Simon added into *The Boxer*? *After changes upon changes, we are more or less the same*."

"We aren't the same, though, are we? We aren't teenagers any more - and you aren't foot loose, even if you seem to regard yourself as fancy free."

"I know we ain't that young any more… *but in our hearts the dreams are still the same*, to quote Mary Hopkin."

"I wish you'd use your own words sometimes, Nigel. You can't hide away behind song lyrics all your life."

"I'm sorry - I thought it was one of my endearing little personality traits."

"It can be - but it can also be a little irritating."

"I do apologise - I'll keep quiet if I'm annoying you."

"Please don't go all petulant on me, Nigel - you keep coming up with these platitudes that don't mean anything in real life - the dreams are great but the reality is that you're going to go back to London and I'm going to go back to my parents' on my own. Then in a week or so term will have started and we'll be back to having surreptitious meetings whenever your wife's back is turned."

"It's turned most of the time, actually."

"So you say but I hate the fact that we can't just be together like normal people."

"What's made you change so suddenly? You were as right as rain a few minutes ago."

"Nothing's happened: I've had a wonderful time but the days' wearing on and I know that it's all got to come to an end, very soon."

"Don't spoil the day now, Sally."

"I'm not trying to spoil it. I can't help it - I just feel like I'm sliding into a slough of despond all of a sudden."

She pulled away from him and sat up, staring at the river, clearly lost in thoughts. He knew that the mood of the afternoon had changed - his melancholy had lost its charm and felt more and more oppressive as the silence lengthened.

Several times he attempted a weak joke or tried to start another conversation but she barely responded and made it clear that she wanted to be left alone with her thoughts, so he decided to keep his silence too.

Eventually she took his hand.

"I'm sorry if I've gone all miserable, Nigel - overwhelmed by a sudden dose of reality I guess. Come on, I'd better get you back to the station, hadn't I?"

They walked wordlessly to her car and the silence continued as they drove back to Cambridge. It was as they approached Magdalene Bridge that he felt the cast-iron certainty that he was losing her and an old Byrds' song called *Lady Friend* began to play over and over in his head. I'm going to have to live without her and survive, he thought to himself.

When they arrived at Cambridge station Sally simply leaned over and kissed him quickly on the cheek. "Thanks for coming, Nigel. It's been a day that I'll never forget. You go back to your family now."

Nigel felt that he ought to say something profound and reassuring but could not think of anything to say other than "Thanks, I'll never forget it either and I hope there'll be many more days like it. Promise you'll keep in touch?"

"I promise but I'm going to be off line for a few days while I'm with my parents. I'll text or e-mail when I get back to London. Off you go now or you'll miss your train."

Nigel hurried off into the station with several quick backward glances in the direction of her car. To his relief, he did not have long to wait for the train and was soon able to sit back and rearrange his thoughts on the day.

It had been wonderful and he was certain that he had never enjoyed anybody's company so much as he had enjoyed Sally's that day. As far as he was concerned, she was his soul mate, the person he wanted to be with - and he felt sure that the feeling was completely mutual. And yet... the situation was fraught with problems.

If he really loved her, could he subject her to the life of guilt and deceit that, realistically, was likely to be all that he could offer her? Had she already come to a decision that afternoon that she would not allow the relationship to develop any further?

Eventually, he gave up trying to analyse the situation any more and, remembering her quip about how he and his friends had always been compiling lists, began mentally to compose a list of his Top Ten All Time Great Songs of Love and Loss:

1. *Simple Twist of Fate* - Bob Dylan
2. *Tangled Up in Blue* - Bob Dylan
3. *I'd rather Go Blind* - Etta James
4. *Me and Bobby McGee* - Janis Joplin
5. *So Long Marianne* - Leonard Cohen
6. *Sleepless Nights* - Emmylou Harris
7. *Empty Chairs* - Don MacLean
8. *Why Does Love Got To Be So Sad?* - Derek and the Dominoes
9. *Still I'm Sad* - Yardbirds
10. *Stay With Me Baby* - Lorraine Ellison

Interesting, he thought, that almost all of them were slow, wistful numbers and that there was no room for the vitriol of *Positively 4th Street* or the triumphalism of *I Will Survive.*

Perhaps there was hope for a long-term relationship with Sally - whatever that meant. He had always guessed that she would never countenance his leaving his family for her, but surely she would see that what they had was really special and to be preserved at all costs.

Chapter 22

During the days that followed, he could think of nothing but Sally and the (to him) unsatisfactory way in which they had taken leave of each other. He found it particularly difficult that there was no one on hand in whom he could confide and wished that he were back at Cambridge, with Pete and Roger always on hand for beer and sympathy.

After three or four days, he called Pete and arranged to meet him that night, in the hope that he might find some solace or, at least, a brief distraction from his preoccupation with Sally.

In recent years they had seen less and less of each other and it saddened him that all that really united them nowadays was their shared past, as a result of which their conversations tended to consist primarily of reminiscences about their student days and the bachelor years in London that followed. It was inevitable therefore that, after updating each other on their families and a discussion on the recent fortunes of the England cricket team, they soon began to talk about various people they had known at Cambridge and to swap anecdotes about each other's youthful indiscretions of yesteryear. This gave Nigel the opportunity to mention with studied casualness that he had visited Cambridge the previous week.

"Great" replied Pete, with mild interest. "What took you there?"

"Oh, you know, just retracing the steps of my youth and all that. I went down Bateman Street on my way from the station-it brought back a few memories."

"No sign of any of the old reprobates from the Class of 'Seventy Five then? All at EuroDisney with their wives and two point four children no doubt. It comes to us all in the end, doesn't it?"

"There is something unsettling about going back there. I always think that Cambridge is like a long-running play-you leave the cast after your three years but the play just carries on without you, as if you'd never been in it.

"I kept looking out for you in your bomber jacket and cowboy boots and for Roger on his lady's bike, with that brown corduroy jacket that he wore whatever the time of year."

"How could I forget it? Do you remember the time that song about the girl on the bicycle came on the radio just when he was going off on his bike and you opened the window and played it really loudly for his benefit? The one that went '*you looked so pretty as you were riding along.*'"

"It was the *Pushbike Song* by the Mixtures-number one in early 1971, I believe. Another of those great one-hit wonders. I'd forgotten that episode but I'll never forget the day we went to look at the house in Bateman Street-remember? It was going home time at the convent and at the Perse girls' school and the street seemed to be awash with nubile sixth formers. We decided there and then that there was nowhere else we would rather live."

"We had Bill Northwick with us, didn't we? And being a bit older than the rest of us he got rather more excited by the young mothers waiting at the gate of the primary school."

Nigel laughed at the memory and then went on, once again with a casualness that was almost forced:

"A propos of which, I did bump into someone who asked to be remembered to you-someone of the female, ah, gender."

"That sounds interesting-who was it? Not that peroxide blonde from Homerton we used to call Kunta Kinte because her roots were always showing? Or that Spanish girl in Shades wine bar whom Roger maintained was the dark one from Baccara? Do you remember? She didn't speak a word of English, so he kept pointing to her and singing yes sir, I can boogie.'

Nigel grinned: " And then he christened here Gleneagles because he said she had a face like an eighteen hole golf course. No, it wasn't any of those: do you remember Sally, that girl from the convent I went out with while we were living in Bateman Street?"

"Yes, I do-a lovely girl, I always thought. Very fit. Whatever happened to her?"

"She seems to have had quite an interesting life; she spent quite a few years working in India and now she's teaching in Ealing. She hasn't changed that much. Oh, and she's never married, amazingly enough."

Pete laughed: "Poor girl: I seem to remember that you dumped her for some old slapper back home who then didn't quite, er, come up to expectations. That was what happened, wasn't it? I must admit that

I quite fancied her myself - Sally I mean, not the Dudley Slag - and had half a mind to ask her out once you'd finished with her, except that in those days my ego wouldn't allow me to make do with shop-soiled goods-or, to be more precise, with your cast-offs. Anyway, where did you run into her?"

"Oh, just walking along King's Parade-it was an amazing coincidence" he lied glibly, before the need to unburden himself became too strong.

"Actually, that's not strictly true-in fact, it's not true at all. I'd arranged to meet her there."

"How come?"

"I found her details on the Friends Reunited website and dropped her an e-mail; she replied and eventually we arranged to meet in London.... Then somehow, over the school holidays the meetings became more and more frequent and...we found that we'd become rather fond of each other."

Pete said nothing, so Nigel went on:

"When we met in Cambridge, we drove out to Houghton Mill-you wouldn't remember but we had cycled there from Cambridge once-and had a wonderful day together. Everything was perfect, but then towards the end she seemed to pull away from me somehow and I just sensed that she was going cold on me. It's hard to explain but it had all been so idyllic, yet I came away feeling as though I'd lost her.

"I haven't been able to talk to her since, because she's been staying with her parents in Cambridge but I can't stop thinking about her.

"I've got myself into a bit of a fix, haven't I?"

Pete was silent for a few moments, then replied: "Are you asking my advice?"

"Not really, Pete, but all counsel gratefully received I guess-particularly if it's what I want to hear."

"You know what I'm going to say, don't you? You've got to run a mile from this 'situation' before it all goes pear-shaped. You're playing with fire, mate."

Nigel said nothing but Pete laughed shortly then continued: " I can promise you that the Shock And Awe tactics that they used in Iraq will be like a Sunday school picnic compared to your fate when Amanda finds out-and she will find out, Nige."

"That isn't what I wanted to hear" Nigel replied eventually. " I thought that you of all people would understand how I feel.

"I know it's wrong, Pete, but it feels so right-like we're complete and utter soul mates. We've never done more than kiss, so you can't put it down to good old-fashioned lust and debauchery. We just talk about anything and everything and have lots of laughs.... And she is always so interested in me-it's so different from how it is with Amanda."

Pete smiled: " I remember when you first met Amanda-you always reminded me of that song by Rickie Lee Jones, *Chuck E's In Love*-do you remember it? The guy who suddenly starts to 'learn all of his lines' and 'acquires a cool and inspired sort of jazz when he walks'? That's just how you were-and how you've always been every time I've seen you in 'lurve.'

"Okay, so maybe some of the magic has been lost over the years but you just have to work at it.... And if you ran off with Sally, sooner or later the magic would disappear again. That's life, matey-it's not all romantic walks hand in hand along the banks of the Ouse or whatever the river up there is called. Even Roger's begun to realize that now-two divorces and hundreds of thousands of pounds of alimony later."

"I just can't see how I could ever get it back with Amanda, Pete-she just lives for her next big deal and I don't feature at all any more."

Pete sighed: " I've never really got to know Amanda very well and that's a real sadness for me-I'm sure it's my fault as much as anybody else's-but I suspect that she isn't really the Superwoman that you think she is.

"My mother used to do some marriage guidance counselling and she used to say that, in that work, you have to listen not just to what people do say but, equally importantly, to what they don't say. Amanda is a woman who has made a very successful career in a male-dominated world, while doing her best to be a good mother to two teenage children. She may seem completely in control, but I'd be amazed if she didn't have worries and uncertainties of her own, once you scratch beneath the surface."

"Oh, yeah, just like Attila The Hun would be uncertain whether to rape, pillage or plunder. I can really relate to the poor old Visigoths-mind you, Amanda is such a devoted servant of Mammon that the choice for her

Andrew Stilton

would be a straight fifty: fifty between plundering and pillaging.

"Sally is just the opposite-she was brought up in the Catholic church and has a strong faith of her own, but she obviously has a real conscience and sometimes seems to be tormented by guilt about what we are doing-even though we have not officially broken any commandments yet. What I don't understand, though, is why she should change so suddenly after such an amazing time together."

"I hate to say this, Nige, but I rather think that she's making your decision for you. From what I remember of her-and from how you describe her now-I don't see her being able to live with herself if she thought that she was responsible for wrecking your marriage."

After a long silence, Nigel replied quietly: " I'm afraid that you're probably right, Pete-as I say, I could feel her slipping away from me that afternoon. But it's as though I've started living again since I began to see Sally and I'm not sure that I could face life without her.

"Do you remember the vision of the future which O'Brien gave to Winston in 1984-a boot standing on a human face for ever? That's about how I see the prospect of being manacled to Amanda 'til death us do part."

"Well, then, what's your problem? Some blokes would pay a fortune for that-wasn't it a nice little earner for that Swedish au pair of yours? Naughty Nella, was it?"

Nigel laughed. "Insatiable Ingrid, actually. Trust you to lower the tone."

"Seriously, Nigel, even if things aren't great with Amanda, don't forget your children-they may seem all grown up but they still need you, I'm sure. At the very least, after lumbering her with a name like Galadriel, you owe it to Ria to be there for her."

Afterwards, he reflect that his conversation with Pete had not really helped him very much: what he really wanted was someone to tell him that he should follow his heart and that Sally would be certain to feel the same way. Instead, Pete's words had only served to reinforce the feeling that gnawed away at his heart, that their day together at Houghton Mill was likely to be the end of their brief but unconsummated affair, rather than the start of a new life for both of them.

Chapter 23

He somehow managed to refrain from contacting her for a few more days but, as the start of school term approached, he felt certain that she must have returned to London by then and sent her a tentative e-mail:

To: Sally Peters
From: Nigel Troy
Wondering if you are back yet. I am still on a high after our day at Houghton Mill.
Love
Nigel

She did not reply immediately but, the following evening, his heart leapt when he looked at his e-mails and saw that there was a message from her; when he read it, however, his spirits sank:

To: Nigel Troy
From: Sally Peters
Yes, I am back home. Sorry to have been so long getting in touch.
I would like to send you another e-mail but would like to be certain that you are there and alone before I send it.
Love
Sally

He knew in his heart that this was it-the end of the line-and he could feel a knot beginning to tighten in his stomach as he replied.

To: Sally Peters
From: Nigel Troy
Here and alone.
This sounds ominous

Her reply was more depressing than he had ever imagined:

To: Nigel Troy
From: Sally Peters
Nigel, this is awfully difficult to say but I spent the last week or so doing a lot of soul searching and I have now told Colin that I will marry him.
I love being with you and would love nothing more than to be marrying you but..... You are not free and there's no point in kidding ourselves that we could have a future together - or, at least, a future that does not involve hurting other people and a whole lot of guilt and recrimination.
That's why I think it's best that I marry Colin - I'm sure that I can be happy with him.
I am really, really sorry, but I hope you agree with me deep down.
Lots of love.
Sally

To: Sally Peters
From: Nigel Troy
We've been so happy these last few weeks and the day at Houghton Mill was the most wonderful day of my life - how can you end it now?

To: Nigel Troy
From: Sally Peters
Nigel, it was a wonderful day for me too. I have never felt so close to anyone - and cannot believe that I ever will again.
But when it was getting towards time to go, I began to feel completely overwhelmed by the hopelessness of it all - because you had to go back to your family and I had to go back to my parents' on my own. And that's how it would always be.

I've got to talk to her face-to face, he thought. It's my only chance.

To: Sally Peters
From: Nigel Troy

Sally, we need to meet up to talk.   We can't just end it like this.

To: Nigel Troy
From: Sally Peters
Please don't try to make me change my mind, Nigel.

To: Sally Peters
From: Nigel Troy
Just half an hour, that's all I ask.

To: Nigel Troy
From: Sally Peters
Ok, half an hour. But please don't try to pressurise me.
Tomorrow night?

To: Sally Peters
From: Nigel Troy
7 o'clock at Green Park Tube?

To: Nigel Troy
From: Sally Peters
Against my better judgment, ok.

To: Sally Peters
From: Nigel Troy
xxxxx

He spent the whole of the following day rehearsing the lines that he was going to say to her but, when they met, he could tell from the briefness of her embrace that her mind was made up and that those words were going to be redundant, so they walked into the park without a word until at last he felt obliged to break the silence.

"I know you asked me not to try to make you change your mind but I still don't see how you can marry this Colin if you don't love him."

"Maybe I don't have the same feelings for him as for you but...he's free and you're not."

"But how can you spend the rest of your life with him?"

"I'm not convinced that romantic love is the be-all and end-all and I'm sure we'll get along just fine."

"But what about me?"

"You've got your wife and family."

"I don't have to stay with Amanda."

"Yes you do" she replied sharply.

"Look, I was brought up to know the difference between right and wrong and what would be the point of that if I didn't do the right thing now? I don't want either of us to do any more wrong than we have already."

"Call me cynical, but I rather agree with Bob Dylan in *Brownsville Girl*: people don't do what they believe in, they just do what is most convenient for them and then they repent."

"Did you ever read Brideshead Revisited?"

"No. Why?"

"There's one point when Julia tells Charles (the central character) that he just doesn't understand her anguish at knowing that all the doors of Heaven are closed to her because of their affair. That's exactly how I would feel if you left Amanda for me - like Eve in Paradise Lost."

Looking back later, he realised that that was the moment when he knew for sure that he had lost her-how could he argue with her conscience? Pete had been quite right.

"Colin would have understood how I felt" she went on, and then she saw the hurt look on his face.

"I'm sorry, Nigel. That was unkind."

She smiled for the first time. "Just think of me as Rick telling Ilsa to get on the plane and go with Laszlo"

"You know I always thought Rick made a big mistake and I think you're doing the same."

"We'll always have Paris."

"I don't want Paris-it's being here now with you that I want."

"Please don't, Nigel. This is hard enough for me as it is."

This is it, he thought to himself, feeling on the verge of tears-the point of no return. Best to be as gracious as possible-if you loved her you would try not to spoil whatever happiness she might feel at marrying this character.

"Okay, okay. I'll respect your decision but I can't stand the thought of losing you. Have you fixed a date?"

"Saturday 25th October - the start of half term."

"He doesn't hang about does he, old Col?

"Sorry, I don't mean to be unkind about him - my thoughts are all over the place."

She stopped walking, drew her to him and let him kiss her lips.

"This is so hard but I know it's the right thing. If you'd been free, it would have been different, I promise."

"Freedom's just another word for nothing left to lose."

"I'd better go, Nigel. Take care."

"You too-what can I say? I hope it all works out for you…and think of me whenever you hear *Angel Wine*."

"I will, I promise. Lots of love."

She kissed him quickly on the cheek and then turned and walked quickly away to the Tube without a backward glance, exactly as she had done on the night of the Queen's Silver Jubilee.

Chapter 24

The rest of that month passed in a daze: he seemed to glimpse Sally's face on every crowded Tube, on every busy street and on a couple of occasions he went back to the spot in Green Park where they had picnicked, hoping against hope that she would be there too. The weather had broken and it was virtually unrecognisable as the place where he had felt so happy just a few months previously.

At least, he had been delivering the same lectures for so many years that he could run through them more or less on auto-pilot, while his family seemed so wrapped up in their own lives, as ever, that nobody seemed to notice if he seemed even more distracted than usual.

So preoccupied was he that during the first few days of term he failed to notice the conspiratorial smiles that Tammy was bestowing in his direction and it was only when he did contrive to detect the hurt look on her face after he absent-mindedly walked right past her without acknowledging her existence that he remembered the episode of the text message and realised that she was awaiting some sign of warmth from him.

Clearly, at some point he was going to have to explain himself to her but, he soon decided, that would have to wait until after the day of Sally's impending nuptials-until then, he adopted the cowardly strategy of pretending to be too shy and love-struck to reveal the affection that he was supposed to feel for her.

His mind was still preoccupied with thoughts of Sally and every day (sometimes, several times each day) he would check his mailbox in the forlorn hope that there might be a message from her but all he ever found was the usual unsolicited junk-until one evening when he received mail from an unexpected quarter.

To: Nigel Troy
From: Heather Crowle

Hello, Nigel! Remember me??
It seems a long time since we have spoken - how are you keeping?
Heather

He could not resist replying and, despite (or was it because of?) his blackness of mood, the exchanges gradually grew more frequent and more flirtatious.

To: **Heather Crowle**
From: **Nigel Troy**
I am fine, thanks. Not looking forward to going back to work - not sure I told you that I am a university lecturer, which means that I get very long holidays (the only perk of the job).
How are you?
Nigel

To: **Nigel Troy**
From: **Heather Crowle**
I am OK, too, ta. I had a few problems with my computer over the summer - you don't lecture in IT by any chance do you? You'd be very welcome to come and power me up any time!!

To: **Heather Crowle**
From: **Nigel Troy**
Afraid I lecture in tax - nothing so practical.
My IT skills are very rough and ready-it's all I can do to find the on/off switch.
Nigel

To: **Nigel Troy**
From: **Heather Crowle**
Rough and ready??!! Mmm, Sounds good to me. I bet you could turn me on!!
How is your mouse control??
Heather

*To: **Heather Crowle***
*From: **Nigel Troy***
I fear I lack the necessary manual dexterity...

*To: **Nigel Troy***
*From: **Heather Crowle***
I can't believe that, Nigel???

*To: **Heather Crowle***
*From: **Nigel Troy***
It's true - in my youth there were no Game Boys or Play Stations to hone these skills on - I was a hot shot at Table Soccer, though.

*To: **Nigel Troy***
*From: **Heather Crowle***
It's a pity I didn't get to know you in Dinard - you would soon have forgotten all about Subbuteo, I promise you!!

*To: **Heather Crowle***
*From: **Nigel Troy***
Another "What if"!

*To: **Nigel Troy***
*From: **Heather Crowle***
You wouldn't have been disappointed - the Shrewsbury Rugby Club weren't!! (Just kidding – it was only the front row!)
It's never too late - how do you fancy a visit to Wales? The nights are drawing in here...

*To: **Heather Crowle***
*From: **Nigel Troy***
I would love to but I don't get back to the Midlands very often and where you are doesn't seem very accessible from London.
Nigel

To: *Nigel Troy*
From: *Heather Crowle*
I'll show you my tattoo!!
Heather

To: *Heather Crowle*
From: *Nigel Troy*
Sounds intriguing - may I ask where it is?
N

To: *Nigel Troy*
From: *Heather Crowle*
That would be telling... but it's where the sun doesn't shine very often!!!

Heather
To: *Heather Crowle*
From: *Nigel Troy*
Even more intriguing - what is it of?
N

To: *Nigel Troy*
From: *Heather Crowle*
The Welsh Rugby Team emblem - the Three Feathers.
I hope that tickles your fancy!!
Heather

To: *Heather Crowle*
From: *Nigel Troy*
Consider my fancy well and truly tickled.
Was it painful?

To: *Nigel Troy*
From: *Heather Crowle*
It was quite painful - my (now ex!!!) husband wanted me to have it done and I agreed just to keep the peace. I am not even Welsh!

I would love to meet you, Nigel - perhaps I'll turn up at one of your lectures, sit quietly at the back and then suddenly stand up and flash my tattoo so you'd know it was me!

To: Heather Crowle
From: Nigel Troy
In my classes, you'd stand out if you did <u>not</u> have a tattoo.
I have been reading a novel about Julius Caesar and it describes his first meeting with Cleopatra - she had herself presented to him rolled up in a carpet, which her servants then unrolled to reveal her wearing very little indeed. That strikes me as a dramatic first meeting.

To: Nigel Troy
From: Heather Crowle
You provide the carpet....

To: Nigel Troy
From: Heather Crowle
Nigel! Guess what ??!! I am coming to London next Thursday with some girlfriends for a few days.
Come and see me and see what you missed back in 1973!! I will be staying in the Medlicott Hotel in Paddington.
See you Thursday at 7 o'clock in the hotel bar – no excuses accepted!
Love Heather

To: Heather Crowle
From: Nigel Troy
How will I recognize you? Will the tattoo be on view?

To: Nigel Troy
From: Heather Crowle
The tattoo comes later!!
I am 5 ft. 6' with blonde hair-quite short (I can't afford a big bottle on what they pay me!!)

To: Heather Crowle

From: Nigel Troy
I will be carrying an umbrella and a rolled-up copy of the Times....

To: Nigel Troy
From: Heather Crowle
Wot no carpet??

To: Heather Crowle
From: Nigel Troy
Not very practical on the Tube!
See you Thursday.

To: Nigel Troy
From: Heather Crowle
I can't wait!   Must go now-it's getting a bit nippy sitting around in my next-to-nothings....

To: Heather Crowle
From: Nigel Troy
Mmmmmm. Pity you don't have a web cam...

To: Nigel Troy
From: Heather Crowle
Naughty boy! Be good (until Thursday!!).
Love Heather
xxxx

Chapter 25

Looking back after the event, Nigel concluded that, if called upon to explain to a jury his conduct in turning up at the Medlicott Hotel at the appointed time, his plea in mitigation could only be that the balance of his mind must have been totally and utterly disturbed by what had happened with Sally-although, in truth, he may also have been motivated by a desire to prove his heterosexuality to Heather on Jane's behalf and also by a sense of adventure which had long lain dormant but which had been awakened by his trysts with Sally.

Whatever the explanation, he duly rolled up as arranged, to see a forty-something bottle blonde in a short denim skirt and a crop top (which she later told him that she had borrowed from her daughter) sitting on a stool at the bar.

He was expecting someone large and voluptuous and so was surprised to find that she was extremely slim. They greeted each other awkwardly (he shaping up to shake her hand while she put her arm round his neck) and then sat side-by-side on a sofa, sipping their drinks (he had ordered a pint of bitter while Heather had asked for a brandy and Babycham).

Somehow he found that talking face-to-face was not as easy as flirting by e-mail, although she was chatty and outgoing from the outset, so he mainly listened while Heather did the talking.

"Is Kylie-Shania your only one?" he asked tamely.

"Oh no. Limahl's nineteen and at college and Stockard's fifteen-doing her G.C.S.E.s next year. We had Kylie-Shania to try to save our marriage but it didn't work.

"He was a Capricorn" she added, as if that explained everything. "We get on okay now though."

"How long have you been divorced?"

"Three years now. I went back to my maiden name when Dave moved in with his new partner-she's okay actually. She's an Aquarius."

"Yes, that would make a difference" he muttered gamely. "Who's got the children now?"

"Lim's at college like I said, but the other two are staying with their Dad. I'm quite lucky-Dave has them quite often and my Mom lives quite near and so I can leave them with her when I want a night out on the town with my girlfriends."

"Not the Shrewsbury Rugby Club these days?"

"Given half a chance.... When was it we were in France, Nigel?"

"August 1973."

"Wow, that's terrifying. I was fifteen then-sweet and innocent and still to be kissed...well I was fifteen anyway. I can remember taking a brown duffel bag with me and that I'd written 'Much Wenlock Boot Boys Rule, OK?'on it. I was really into skinheads in those days-I can't begin to imagine why now. I was always listening to Desmond Dekker and stuff like that."

"So what's your all time favourite record?"

"*Typical Girls* by the Slits, I think."

"The Slits? I've never heard of them."

"You must've done-they were an all-girl Punk band. Brilliant, they were."

"Nice name."

"You must have heard of them: the lead singer was called Ari Upp and she used to wear a tiny little skirt with Jubilee knickers underneath. I went to see them live once and went out and bought a pair specially for the occasion."

"Were you really into Punk in a big way?"

"Of course. When I left school and went to college I started going out with this punk called Gordon and I had my hair bleached and started wearing fishnet stockings and safety pins all over my face. He was a nice bloke, that Gordon-but he had one of those Mohican haircuts and the spikes could be a bit painful at times."

"I can imagine-best not go there, I think. I was never really into Punk-I liked some of it, but I think I was afraid that it would displace Led Zeppelin and Bob Dylan and all the music I really liked. And I don't think the Slits ever played Cambridge."

"You should have gone to art school like me-you didn't know I went to college, did you?"

No, I didn't." He tried to keep the surprise out of his voice. "Where did you go?"

"In Wolverhampton. I dropped out after two years though-worst mistake I ever made...apart from marrying a Capricorn, that is."

"So why did you give it up?"

"I dunno now. I'd split up with Gordon and that was part of it-he went off with another girl, just like in that song, *Jilted John*, so I got some spray paint and wrote 'Gordon is a moron' all over his moped. The people at the college didn't like that very much but as much as anything I just wanted to earn some money-so I packed in college and worked as a hotel receptionist for a bit, which meant the end of the spiky hair and the safety pins.

"I started spending my money on going out clubbing with Jane every weekend-and buying those tight black pants that girls used to wear in those days."

"You mean the ones that looked like they'd been sprayed on? I don't remember them at all."

"I'm sure you do-we used to wear them and sparkly boob tubes-except that I never had the boobs to go with mine. Were you a keen clubber, Nigel?"

"Not really. I never liked Disco music-it all sounded the same to me and every record seemed to last for ever. Anyway, do you fancy something to eat?"

"That would be nice, thanks."

"Shall we go into the restaurant?" he asked, in the hope of steering her away from the 'Lite Bite' menu on the bar, which contained a list of (to him) singularly unappetising dishes, all no doubt awash with mayonnaise.

"I'd be happy with the bar menu" she answered, to his disgust. "Must watch my figure at my age."

Heather ordered a dubious-looking salad, while Nigel contented himself with the Crispy Potato Skins In A Spicy Sauce and made a note to call in at his local chip shop on the way home.

"It sounds like you and Jane had a lot of fun together" he continued once they had ordered.

"Oh yeah, you bet, we certainly knew how to party."

She gave a long sigh.

"It's strange: I was always the adventurous one but it's Jane who's living in exotic places while I've wound-up working in a supermarket, a few miles from my Mom and Dad."

She was silent for a few moments and then touched his knee very lightly. "I can still be very adventurous, though, when I'm in the right mood, I promise you."

"I never doubted it for a second" he laughed, rather nervously.

"Anyway, Nigel" she went on as their food arrived looking as unappetising as it had sounded "what made you remember Jane after so long?"

"I don't know.... I was just thinking about that holiday in Dinard and the people from my school who were on the trip and then I remembered the party from Shropshire who had livened things up a bit. For some reason, Jane's name had always stuck in my memory.

"Not that I spent much time with her" he added quickly. "So what happened to her between Dinard and meeting her chap in Corfu?"

"Well, not long after we got back from Dinard she started going out with a bloke from school called Gary - she always claimed that he seduced her in the back of his passion wagon, as she used to call it-actually, it was his dad's Austin Allegro-while *Billy Don't Be A Hero* was playing on the radio. They got engaged pretty soon but she never seemed in a great hurry to marry him - used him as a bit of a doormat really.   Anyway, eventually we went on this holiday to Corfu and she met this Kostas on the second night and never went home. Not a great holiday for me being left on my own most of the time... but I'm pretty good at making my own amusements, Nigel."

She paused for a few moments: "Hey, I know what I meant to ask you: did you ever find out who that weirdo was - you know, the bloke she fancied in Dinard who just wanted to talk about football?"

"No, I've no idea. There were some pretty weird and not-so wonderful people at my school, though. It's a miracle that I turned out so normal."

"I can't remember much about the holiday except that there was a disco one night and I wound up dancing with a real jerk - very handsome he was but all he kept saying was that nobody expects the Spanish Inquisition."

Nigel smiled. "Ah, that would have been Rick Powis. He's a Catholic priest now. Only joking - he's a doctor, apparently. That's a scary thought - I wouldn't let him within half a mile of any part of my anatomy."

"I was quite keen to let him near all of mine, I remember, but he got on my nerves after a bit. Anyway, Nigel, I've been talking about myself all evening but I don't know anything about you-did you say that you were a lecturer on tax? Is that exciting?"

"No, it's about as unexciting as it's possible for any human activity to be, I'm afraid. I must have done something very bad in a past life. Perhaps I'll come back as a cockroach next time".

"Sounds like bad karma to me" was Heather's enigmatic response. "Have you always been a lecturer?"

"No, I trained as a solicitor and practiced as a tax lawyer but I've have been teaching for about 15 years."

"Mmm. Soliciting sounds a lot more fun! I think I'd be rather good at that, don't you?"

Nigel groaned inwardly and wondered how many times he had heard someone make that rather weak joke, while Heather embarked on the story of her marriage to Dave the ill-starred Capricorn.

Eventually she lapsed into silence and stretched and yawned:

"I'm going to have to get out of these heels, Nigel: let's go up to my room for a nightcap. I'll go on ahead while you settle up. It's room 101".

"What's your room like?"

"It's okay now but I had to get reception to rearrange it. Bad feng shui - you shouldn't sleep with a door behind you.

"Mirrors on the ceiling are okay though" she grinned as she tottered off on her high heels, leaving Nigel to pay the bill and think about how the evening had gone.

He had to admit that he had enjoyed her company far more than he had anticipated: he had expected her to be rather vacuous and boring but, he decided, she was simply another forty-something who had not made the most of the opportunities she had been given and was now tormented by "what ifs?" just as he was-somebody else who, in the words of Pink Floyd, had missed the starting gun.

At least, he thought, she wasn't going to give up without fighting back against the depredations of time and he admired her for that.

Perhaps it was these warm feelings or the effect of a couple of pints of Directors on an empty stomach ("Lite Bites" did not count, as far as Nigel was concerned) that made him he ignore the Orwellian associations of the room number, stroll up the stairs to the first floor and knock on the door.

It opened silently and he was surprised to find the room in total darkness and apparently empty until he heard her whisper, "sorry Cleopatra couldn't make it, Nigel, so you'll have to make do with me", whereupon the light came on and he found himself confronted by Heather draped in an iridescent pink rug.

"Do you like it?" she asked. "I bought it on the street market today, especially for the occasion."

"Er, yes, very tasteful" was about all he could say before she let it fall to the floor, leaving her wearing just a pale blue thong and a lascivious smile.

"No asps, look" she announced as she put her arms round him and drew him to her. "Enjoy!"

It was only then that he realised that she was not just slim but almost painfully thin - so much so that as they embraced, the pressure of her rib cage made him feel as though he was having a close encounter with a toast rack.

"Do you like my tattoo?" she asked, turning round and pointing to a small indeterminate mark on her lower back, just below her waist, which looked rather like a bar code.

"Er, yes, how gorgeous!" he managed to reply. "Are they the Prince Of Wales' Feathers?"

"That's right-if only he knew where his feathers had been! It would make those ears of his burn. I'm thinking of having another one-maybe the cross of St. George this time. Where do you think it would look best?"

He had no time to reply because she suddenly swung round to face him; her tongue was in his ear and then in his mouth, while her hands were undoing (and removing) his clothes with remarkable dexterity. As she kissed him firmly on the mouth, he closed his eyes and pretended that it was Sally. Soon he was kissing her with a passion that surprised him, although he felt that the experience might have been rendered more

209

pleasurable if it were not for the hint of mayonnaise on her breath - a remnant of her Lite Bite in the bar.

As she undid his belt, he realised with a shock that it was over 20 years since a woman other than Amanda had had the dubious pleasure of seeing him in his underpants and tried to put the thought out of his mind - this in itself was difficult as he remembered with some embarrassment that he was wearing a pair that Matt had bought him for his birthday, with a picture of Homer Simpson on the front, pointing towards his nether regions and saying "doh!"

Eventually she pulled him down onto the bed and fell on top of him. He caressed her shoulders, and then began to run his fingers up and down her back. It was as he traced them along the protruding ridge of her spine and the felt the thinness of her shoulder blades that he suddenly knew that he could not be unfaithful to Amanda with Heather - although whether this was due to a renewed awareness of the sanctity of marriage or the fact that he found a semi (in fact, more than semi) - naked Heather singularly unappealing, he could not say.

There are more curves on a skateboard, he thought to himself and he gently pushed her off him and began to mumble something about having to make himself more comfortable for the long night of passion ahead, before making a dash for the open door of the bathroom. Heather attempted a very passable rugby tackle which led to the demise of the Homer Simpson underpants but he finally managed to extricate himself and dive into the bath room, throwing a quick "back in a moment, darling" in Heather's direction. He heard her reply by throwing herself onto the bed and shouting something about not keeping a girl waiting.

Once in the sanctuary of the bathroom, he took stock of the situation.

What would James Bond do in his position? He wondered, but then realised that Ursula Andress emerging from the waves in a bikini was more his style and that it was inconceivable that 007 would ever be trapped in a hotel bedroom with a sexually voracious stick insect.

What would the Famous Five do? George would be rescued by Timmy the dog, while Julian and Dick would just shin down a drainpipe and escape. Sadly, he thought, his shinning days were well behind him but, opening the window, he saw that it opened onto a light well and that the ground was not too far below. The question was how to get down there.

Looking around in desperation, he saw that there was a generous supply of towels in the bathroom and, by knotting them together, he was able to make a serviceable rope, which, he could see, would be long enough to get him within a few feet of the ground. He quickly tied one end of his "rope" to the towel rail and lowered the other end through the open window. He was just about to climb down when he noticed that he was completely naked but for a pair of Mr Happy socks.

Salvation was, however, at hand in the form of the shower curtain and he quickly unhooked it and then used the hooks to form it into a makeshift toga. Thus clad, he gently began to climb down.

On the way down, he found himself humming *Fifty Ways to Leave Your Lover* and reflected that he had obviously found the Fifty First: it was all very well for Jack and Stan - they just had to slip out the back or make a new plan, while he found himself dressed in a plastic toga and climbing precariously out of a hotel window.

Two thirds of the way down, he felt the towel rail come away from the wall, but so slowly that he was able to drop gently to the ground and escape to freedom through a door and along a short corridor which, it transpired, led him straight into the hotel kitchens.

There he was confronted by an oriental-looking chef brandishing a carving knife, who reminded him alarmingly of something out of Apocalypse Now. Putting on what he hoped sounded a suitably gruff military voice, Nigel barked out "Anti-Terrorist Squad... Suspicious Package... Under Cover... Hush Hush" and pushed quickly past the startled looking chef, down a further corridor and into the reception area, where he found himself facing a middle-aged concierge who regarded him suspiciously and asked, in an icy voice "can I help you, sir?"

In a moment of sheer inspiration, Nigel calmly asked "Which way to the Charity Gala Roman Orgy evening - or have I got the wrong venue?" and, on being told that he must have got it wrong, walked out into the street with as much dignity as he could muster.

He headed for the Tube, before realising that his cash and credit cards were still in his trouser pocket and that his trousers were somewhere in Heather's hotel room. Not having the slightest intention of going to retrieve them, he pondered how to get home.

He toyed with the idea of trying to earn a fast buck by pretending to be part of an avant garde street theatre group and re-enacting the death of Julius Caesar, the performance culminating in an accusing *Et Tu Brute!* addressed to some innocent bystander or, alternatively, a Kenneth Williams style *"Infamy! Infamy! They've all got it in for me"*-but, either way, he decided that his thespian skills were distinctly lacking and that Londoners would most likely just step over his prostrate body on their way to the escalators or rob of him of his Mr. Happy socks.

Seeing a busker at the entrance to the Tube station, he had yet another moment of inspiration: remembering that he had a good tenor singing voice, he decided to try earning the fare home by busking. Given his current state of attire, something with a Roman theme was clearly called for, but the only song he could think of was *Little Does She Know* by the Kursaal Flyers which, he recalled, contained a line about a girl dropping her bikini, *"the one I bought for her in Rome."*

Eventually he decided upon a more general Italian theme and so gave a rendition of Rene and Renato's *Save Your Love For Me*, (in which they sang *"Save Your Love for Roma and for me"*) followed by Joe Dolce's seminal work from 1981, *Shaddapayaface*, at the end of which he had earned the princely sum of 18p.

In sheer desperation he then tried *Don't Worry, Be Happy* which seemed to strike a chord with the assembled populace and at the end of it he found £3.18 on the floor in front of him - enough for the fare home and to buy a newspaper as well.

On the train, his fellow passengers soon made it clear that they regarded him as a (hopefully) harmless lunatic - to be ignored in the hope of avoiding becoming embroiled in conversation with him- so his journey was rather uneventful. Nevertheless it was with some relief that he walked up the path to his own front door... and realised that his key was still in Room 101 of the Medlicott Hotel.

After ringing the bell, he stood on the step whistling nonchalantly and trying to pretend that it was the most natural thing in the world for him to be standing there dressed in a floral plastic toga and a (by now rather grubby) pair of socks and looking, he decided, as if he had just stepped off the set of a low budget remake of Up Pompeii.

As it turned out, he need not have worried as Matt opened the door without even glancing at him, muttered "hi, Dad, Chelsea are losing one-nil" and then returned to his football, leaving Nigel a free run to go upstairs and dress.

His priority then was to put a stop on his various credit cards, which he assumed he would never see again.

This in itself proved to be one of life's more irritating tasks as each call followed the same script.

"Welcome to our credit cardholders' emergency number. Please note that your call may be recorded for training purposes. If you are using a touchtone keypad, press the star key now."

"Are you looking for a loan? We are able to offer our valued cardholders a loan of up to £10,000 at an APR of only 8%. Press 1 now for more information.

"Buying a house? We can offer mortgages at unbeatable fixed or variable rates. Press 2 for more details. Loans are subject to status. Your home may be at risk if you fail to keep up with the repayments.

"Otherwise, stay on the line for more options.

"If you have a query about your credit card statement, press 3.

"If you are calling about a card renewal, press 4.

"If your card has been lost or stolen, press 5.

"Thank you. All of our operators are busy, but your call is important to us."

There would then be a pause of 30 seconds while Santana's *Black Magic Woman* played tinnily in the background, then:

"Thank you. Our operators are still busy, but your call is important to us, please hold.

"Why not apply for an additional card for your partner? Press 6 now for more information."

At that point, Santana would then give way to the Enya music which, during the early 1990s, the BBC had used as the background to every sequence of amusing moments from Wimbledon - even now, Nigel could not listen to it without seeing, in his mind's eye, Boris Becker doing a Fosbury Flop over the net or Gabriel Sabatini pouting at a recalcitrant blackbird.

"Our operators are still busy, but your call is important to us, please hold."

More Enya, then some Phil Collins until at last he would hear a (somewhat less disembodied) voice say in a strong Geordie accent: "Good evening, my name is Jason, how can I help you?"

He would then explain the reason for his call.

On the first occasion, partly in an attempt to be friendly and partly in sheer relief at finding himself speaking to a human being at last he commented:

"Nice weather for the time of year isn't it?" and received the answer "yes, sir, it was a good monsoon this year too."

"I beg your pardon?"

"Yes, sir, here in Bangalore we had 24 inches of rain in one week."

"Bangalore?"

It was then that he realised that he was speaking to an off shore call centre. "I don't suppose they've taught you the words of *The Fog On The Tyne* have they?"

There was no reply so he went on: "Has anybody there been taught to speak with a Birmingham accent?"

"Oh, yes, sir" Jason replied, dropping the Geordie accent altogether. My friend Parvati here is known as the South Indian Annie Turtle."

Despite his frustration at the length on time that this apparently simply exercise had taken, he laughed. "You people do your research, don't you? I think you'll find that she was called Amy Turtle but if you ever get Crossroads on satellite TV, take a tip from me and turn if off quickly. Is your name really Jason?"

"No, sir, it is Shiva. But they are telling me that to work in a call centre I have to call myself Jason. Parvati, she is called Chelsea."

"Could be worse - she might have become West Bromwich Albion or Accrington Stanley."

"I am sorry, sir."

"No worries, Shiva - just my attempt at humour. Goodnight."

Eventually, exhausted by his escape from the clutches of Heather and his battle with off-shore call centres, he made himself a cup of coffee and decided to retire to the study to listen to the relaxing sounds of Carole

King's *Tapestry* and to think back over the events of the evening.

En route, however, he met Matt and realised that he had completely forgotten that his son was in the house.

"Hi, Dad. You've been on the phone a long time."

"I seem to have mislaid my wallet and so I had to stop all my credit cards. Complete pain - takes forever."

"Where did you lose it?"

"I went out for a drink with Roger... at the Punch and Judy in Covent Garden... and I must have left it there, I guess." He felt surprisingly guilty at lying to his son and could feel his cheeks becoming more and more flushed.

"Anyhow" he changed the subject abruptly, "how did the football finish up?"

"One all. Chelsea equalised with a penalty in injury time - not a bad result."

"I wonder when they're playing Wolves at Stamford Bridge. We should try and get tickets."

"Yeah, right, Dad, that would be cool."

"Last time I saw Wolves play Chelsea" Nigel went on, ignoring the evident lack of enthusiasm in his son's voice, "must have been about thirty years ago. That was a great Chelsea side with Peter Osgood and Alan Hudson - and Peter Bonetti in goal. What a team - they partied hard too, by all accounts.

"Wolves were too good for them, though" he reminisced. "We won two nil. Dave Wagstaffe gave Chopper Harris a real roasting all afternoon and Dougan scored the goals - both of them headers."

Matt laughed. "You know what, Dad? You're getting like those old buffers you always used to laugh at, who can remember something that happened fifty years ago but can't remember something you told them ten minutes ago."

Nigel smiled as his son continued. "Seriously, though, don't get your hopes up over the Chelsea-Wolves game. The world has moved on a bit in the last thirty years and Wolves haven't caught up with it yet.

"Anyway, I'd better be going to bed. See you tomorrow, Dad."

Wow, he thought to himself as he drank his coffee, for a couple of minutes back there we made a passable attempt at a conversation. Perhaps I do the boy an injustice and maybe he quite likes me after all.

Feeling his mood beginning to improve, he began to think back over the events of the evening.

Sally was gone from his life forever, there was little doubt about it, but tonight he had come close to throwing everything else away. For the first time in many years, he felt thankful that he had a wife who worked all hours and a family who were out (his daughter) or (most of the time, anyway) treated him as a non-person (Matt). He felt a deep sense of relief that none of them could ever find out about the episode with Heather and it was with these thoughts that he went to bed, hoping to forget about the evening's escapades.

His peace was, however, soon shattered by a loud slamming of the front door, which heralded the return of Amanda from the office, very obviously in a black mood and determined to make sure that everybody knew it.

There was only one solution, he quickly decided - and turned the light out, drew the bedclothes over his head and pretended to be asleep.

His wife, however, was in no humour to leave him in peace and proceeded to turn the light on before cursing her firm, her colleagues and her clients in language that would have made a Sergeant Major blush.

"Bad day at the office, dear?" he muttered eventually, in what he hoped were sympathetic tones.

"Just don't ask. Okay?" she answered, before launching into another tirade, at the end of which she astounded him by throwing her office clothes into a crumpled heap on the floor and then jumping into bed beside him.

"You wouldn't believe what's happened: Vijay has been head-hunted by one of the big American firms, Feldstein & Black-no doubt offering him mega-bucks-and tried to walk out today, taking his team with him. We've put them all on garden leave but the IT people were able to get back all his trashed e-mails from the last few weeks-they're still on his hard drive, whatever that means-and it turns out that he's been sending the Americans all his client lists and that he's been e-mailing all his clients and contacts to tell them where he's going and asking them to follow him.

"We've threatened them with an injunction unless they get everything sent back to us and get us a sworn declaration from F&B that they haven't kept copies and we've also threatened to sue F&B if any of his clients follow him there in the next six months. The Grim Reaper is spitting blood, as you can imagine."

Amanda's strident tones jerked him back to the present.

"It makes me sick; we've given him all the resources that he's asked for so that he could build up the Projects team and then as soon as he's offered thirty pieces of silver from somebody else, he's off."

Nigel made sympathetic noises as Amanda went on, in full flow.

"What really bugs me is that for the last few years he's been the Grim Reaper's blue-eyed boy, the epitome of what a BM partner should be-despite the fact that he's just a pompous prima Donna and always plotting away behind the scenes. Trouble is that they don't value loyalty any more-Robert's only interested in the bottom line and can't see beyond the end of his nose."

"Long-sighted, is he, then?" Nigel ventured involuntarily, thinking of Watson's vast proboscis and drawing an unexpected smile from Amanda.

"I'm sorry to go on, Nige, but you know better than anyone how committed I've always been to the firm-and, yes, I know that that has been at the expense of my marriage and my children sometimes-so I feel completely betrayed."

To his amazement, she suddenly tore her clothes off, threw them in a heap on the floor and jumped into bed beside him.

"Some TLC from my husband please" she demanded rather than requested and, in no time at all-and for the second time in the space of a few hours - there was a tongue flicking in and out of his ear. Reflecting that that was one part of his anatomy which was unlikely to need a wash in the foreseeable future, he put all thoughts of Heather, shower curtains and busking out of his mind and allowed himself to enjoy the novelty of being awake in the same bed as his wife - remembering this time to avoid saying anything which might prompt her to go and attend to client business.

Chapter 26

The day of the wedding was a lovely, warm, October day but, as soon as Nigel awoke, he felt as if he were enveloped in a dark cloud of gloom - and his mood was not improved by hearing the strains of *Lonely This Christmas* in his local newsagent's.

What a depressing time of year, he thought to himself. True, it was bright and sunny and the autumn colours were glorious but there was something about the shortening days and lengthening shadows in October that always seemed to him to presage the inevitable slow, dreary decline into winter - whereas a bright February day, for example, always seemed to carry with it the promise of spring and summer. Besides, a sunny day did not suit his mood at all.

Amanda had left early to do some shopping ahead of yet another day in the office, Matt had gone to rugby training and Galadriel had not yet (as he uncharitably thought) crawled out from underneath her stone and so thankfully he was left alone to luxuriate in his own unhappiness. He drank several cups of black coffee while he read the newspaper, then he adjourned to the study and played *Blood On The Tracks* and thought about how different his life might have been if he had been able to spend it with Sally. The time they had spent together in the summer had given him a tantalising glimpse of the happiness that he might have had – and this morning the "what ifs" seemed almost unbearable.

Like, he thought, the condemned man praying for a last-minute reprieve, he decided to check his e-mails in the fond hope that there might be a message from Sally to say that she had decided not to marry Colin after all and wanted to spend the rest of her life with him.

As he scrolled down, however, he was simply confronted by the usual array of spam, to which he began to reply with rather more bitterness than normal.

To: **Nigel Troy**
Subject: **Viagra by male (!) order - Wow!**
As a gentleman of a certain age, do you sometimes feel in need of a little something to help you rise to the occasion? Take advantage of our special offer of a year's supply of Viagra tablets for only £2.50 (plus p&p). Neither you (nor your loved ones!) will be disappointed.
To order, click here without delay.
To be taken off the circulation list, go to <u>www.wow!factor//179643//</u> <u>GAB//489LZ.co.uk</u>

He replied:
Too late - what's the point? Would rather put the money towards a new Max Bygraves record.
Or would it help my peonies to stay upright without stakes if I fed them with this stuff?

N. Troy
To: **Nigel Troy**
Subject: **Cash deposit**
Greetings, Mr Troy.
Allow me to introduce myself: from 1989 to 1998 I was Finance Minister of a West African republic, during which time I deposited sums totalling US$15.0 million in a personal bank account in Amsterdam.
I am writing to you as an individual of reputation and discretion in order to request your assistance in helping me to access these funds.
In return for your assistance you will receive US$8.5 million and will pay me just US$6.5 million.
Please kindly e-mail to me by return your bank account details and your passport number, together with its date and place of issue. The money will then be transferred to your account within one week.
I await your immediate response.
Your obedient servant
Cornelius P. Dicker

He began his reply in the language of Hurree Jamset Ram Singh, one of Billy Bunter's chums from the Greyfriars' Remove in the books that he used to read in his youth (at the time, he thought wistfully, when Jane was getting up close and personal with Gary to the strains of Paper Lace and Heather was scrumming down with the local rugby club).

O esteemed and idiotic Mr Dicker. Your persistfulness is terrific.

But then a wave of anger came over him and he simply added:

Drop dead!

To: **Nigel Troy**
Subject: **Russian Women looking for British Men**
Still looking for that special someone? Then look no further!
Visit us here and find the woman of your dreams.
You can browse through our pictures and bios of beautiful Russian women guaranteed to thaw the heart of a Western man like you.
Click below for the start of a relationship that may last a lifetime.

He was then invited to click on a picture of a dark haired girl with Slavonic features, wearing nothing but a Cossack hat and a welcoming smile.

He was about to reply, when he caught sight of an e-mail with the subject: *Contact from Friends Reunited - Adrian Ablethorpe.*

Although he had no idea who Adrian Ablethorpe was and no wish at all to be reunited with him, he was unable to resist opening the message, in the irrational hope that it might be Sally writing under a nom de plume.

Dear Nigel,

You probably won't remember me from school [nope - you're dead right there, thought Nigel] *as I was a few years younger than you but I really enjoyed reading your notes on Friends Reunited - what an interesting life you have had!*

I work for Sandwell Council's Environmental Health Department, which is pretty exciting, but I have never been a spy or climbed K2!

The reason for contacting you though is that I love the Krankies and wonder if you might be able to get their autographs for me. That would be fandabidozey!!

Yours sincerely,

Adrian Ablethorpe.

He began to pen a trenchant reply:

Dear Adrian

Is irony lost on you? Get a life - take up train spotting or join a Morris Dancing troupe.

In the end, though, he began to feel guilty and contented himself with *Hi, Adrian.*

Of course I remember you-great to hear from you.

It's a long time since I last saw either of the Krankies but I will see what I can do.

Nigel Troy

He sent the replies and then paused to think of what Sally would be doing.

He pictured her leaving the house on Jesus Green with her father and driving to the church, while Colin (whom he loathed on principle) waited impatiently.

Soon she would be walking down the aisle…and then the pair of them would be exchanging their vows….

Hoping to dispel these images, he turned back to his emails to find a message from Heather, which he opened with some trepidation.

To: Nigel Troy
From: Heather Crowle

You little worm! You toe rag! You are like a haemorrhoid on the backside of the human race.

You were happy enough to come up to my room, weren't you? What did you think was going to be on offer? Cocoa?? A bedtime story?

And where did you get those underpants from?

I did recognise you anyway - you were that creepy guy who fancied Jane in Dinard, weren't you? I recognised your pathetic, frightened little face.

Do you know what we nicknamed you? Larry Grayson, because that's who you reminded us of - except he was a bit more macho than you!!

All I can say is that I hope your wife will enjoy reading this.

It was only when he reached the end of the message that he saw with absolute horror that it had been copied to *amanda.*

221

cadogan@bodkinmanners.com, which he knew was indeed Amanda's e-mail address.

But how could she have known this? he wondered, then realised that it would not be difficult to find out her firm simply by keying her name into one of the search engines and that it would then be a simple matter to telephone the firm to obtain her e-mail address. Whatever had impelled him to give his wife's name on the Friends Reunited website?

He thought rapidly: realistically he was likely to have an hour and a half's or may be two hours' grace before Amanda would be in the office and opening her e-mails - somehow he had to make sure that Heather's message was off her screen before then.

The question was: how was he going to do that?

He considered the possibility of calling the recently-reinstated James on a lad-to-lad basis in order to enlist his help - James was likely to be in the office and might have proxy access over Amanda's mailbox. The downside, however, was that he might be so keen to re-ingratiate himself with Amanda that he would spill the beans - and, at the very least, he did not relish the idea of becoming in thrall to James.

He considered the possibility of allowing Amanda to read the message and then blaming it on a new virus -The Hell Hath No Fury Virus with the ability to get into its victims' address books and then send them "woman scorned" e-mails with copies to their wives, but he soon realised that that would be too far-fetched and that the Bodkin Manners IT department would soon disabuse her on that score.

At that point, an alternative means of salvation came to mind. Amanda normally used her lap top when she wanted to access e-mails from home, but occasionally she used an internet-based system that the firm had set up earlier in the year - and did so via their home PC.

Logging onto the Internet, he saw that she had recently added *http:// mail@bodkinmanners.com* to Favourites and guessed that that was the address for remote access to e-mails.

He opened the page, inserted Amanda Cadogan as the user, but then found that to progress further he needed to type in a password.

He frantically tried the words and phrases that seemed to be an obvious choice for her password - her personalised number plate, Matthew, Matt, Galadriel, her date of birth, even his own name - but without success.

There was only one thing for it, he decided - to try to get the number from her.

He dialled her mobile and was relieved to hear her answer it.

"Hi, darling, how are you?"

"Hello, Nigel, what do you want?"

"Just touching base - I've hardly spoken to you this last week. Where are you?"

"In Harvey Nicks, having a bit of retail therapy. Then I've got a heavy afternoon in the office. What are you up to? Drinking coffee and listening to Bob Dylan?"

"No, I've got quite a lot of work to do. I'm struggling, though - I need to get into my university e-mails but I don't use remote access very often and I can't remember my password, so maybe I'll just have to go in early on Monday, instead."

He paused, then added casually:

"I wish I could think of a password that's easy for me to remember but not so obvious that the world and his wife can see all my mail - what do you do?"

She laughed: "You'd be really cross with me, if I told you."

"No, go on, I'm interested" he replied, trying to keep the note of desperation out of his voice.

"Well, I remember you telling me that in your youth you were known as Doris Troy and that's what I use as my password - I can't imagine that anybody at BM will ever have heard of her, whoever she was."

For the first time in his life, Nigel felt truly thankful for his school nickname. He felt that if Ms. Troy were with him now, he would smother her in kisses from head to toe and he vowed then and there that if he were able to intercept the message from Heather, he would go straight out and buy every Doris Troy CD to be found in London (which he guessed, was a task which was unlikely to be of Herculean proportions).

"Great idea - must try that one myself" he enthused. "See you later then."

"Oh, OK, bye, Nigel" Amanda replied in rather a puzzled-sounding voice, but all that Nigel cared about was whether he could now get into her mailbox.

He typed in *Doris Troy* but, to his horror, received a message that the password was not recognised. He tried *DorisTroy*, *Doris-Troy* and *Doris.Troy* and, finally, *doristroy*, which miraculously got him onto the system, where he found Heather's e-mail sitting, apparently unopened, in Amanda's mailbox.

He was about to delete it, when it occurred to him that Heather might be tempted to try further communications if she did not hear from Amanda and so he quickly typed and sent a reply in Amanda's name:

> ***To: Heather Crowle***
> ***From: Amanda Cadogan***
> *Dear Ms. Crowle*
> *Thank you for copying me into this e-mail: rest assured that my husband will be feeling the full force of my wrath.*
> *However, your own conduct in this episode leaves much to be desired and, if my husband or I receive any further communications from you (written or oral, electronic or otherwise) I will sue you for every penny you have got for enticement and loss of consortium.*
> *I will also issue proceedings for injunctive relief to prevent any further contact.*
> *Yours faithfully*
> *Amanda Cadogan*
> *Solicitor of the Supreme Court*

Having sent it, he remembered to trash it from sent items and then to trash the incoming e-mail, before deleting both of them from Amanda's trash bin.

After all the exertion, he slumped in his chair and checked his watch, to see that it was already 12.30. Sally would be married by now, he was sure - he pictured her leaving the church on Colin's arm, walking through a beaming congregation of friends and relatives to the waiting photographers, while the church bells pealed exultantly.

He had planned to play *When The Levee Breaks* at full volume at midday but it was too late and anyway he felt in the mood for some music that was quieter and more reflective, so he plumped for *Going To California* instead.

Going to California with an aching heart...
Someone told me there's a girl out there with love in her eyes and flowers in her hair.

He closed his eyes and thought of Sally by the river at Houghton...

He was so lost in the music that he did not hear the door open but then he felt his daughter's hands on his shoulders and heard her say softly: "it's today, is it, Dad?"

He was too surprised to reply but sat there in silence until she said: "You've done the right thing."

"What do you mean?" he asked, feeling the blood drain from his face.

"You know what I mean" she said quietly.

Abruptly he turned the music off, then turned to face her. "How did you know?"

"Kieran and his mate, Marcus, saw you together - in a park. I think. Marcus is from Cambridge and his parents are, like, friends of her parents. So, like, a million to one chance, I suppose."

He sat there in stunned silence as she continued.

"You're not a natural deceiver, either, Dad. You kept leaving the computer logged on with all your e-mails there for everybody to read - don't worry, I've deleted them all now."

"Thanks, Ria. Your mother doesn't know, does she?" he asked, the panic all too evident in his voice.

"I don't think so - you know what she's like, she doesn't read anything that doesn't, like, relate to corporate deals. She might begin to suspect that something was up if she saw you, like, wandering round Islington in a shower curtain, though."

Nigel sat bolt upright. "How do you know about that?"

"Matt told me all about it. He pretended he was too preoccupied with the football to notice but he was just trying to save you embarrassment. He can be quite sensitive when he wants to be, can our Matthew."

She giggled: "It must have been a sight for sore eyes, though - whatever will the neighbours say?"

"Back in Dudley, the lace curtains would have been twitching and it would have been the talk of the market place by now. Here, you could die in the street and the neighbours wouldn't give a monkey's."

She touched his arm lightly and he sat in silence for some time.

225

"I don't know what to say, Ria" he said at last. "I feel like I've betrayed you all. Are you sure Mum doesn't know?"

"I'm sure she doesn't, Dad. I think we'd all have known it if she had - you especially. The Exocets would have been, like, raining down on you by now. I'm not going to tell her and I'm sure Matt won't either.

"My silence comes at a price, though, Dad. You can, like, do something in return - phone Mum and arrange to take her out to dinner tonight."

He visibly blanched. "What, me? Take your mother out for dinner? Just the two of us? With no clients? She'd never agree."

"Of course she would. You think she's so tough and - what's that word? Focused? - But she's really, like, struggling at the moment. That client of hers you can't stand - Harry? Barry? - has someone wanting to buy his company and he's her biggest client. It would be a big fee for her but she reckons it would be like selling off the family silver."

"How do you know all this? She's never mentioned it to me?"

"Matt told me - she talks to him because she thinks he's just a thick rugby player who doesn't understand anything, but that's not fair. Anyhow, she's really worried about what she would do if this Barry guy sold out."

Nigel sighed: "seems like Matthew knows more about what's going on in his parents' lives than either of them do - that speaks volumes, doesn't it? Alright, I promise that I will ask your mother to come out for dinner with me."

"Good. And I've got something here to cheer you up a little - it's the best I can do" she added, handing him two slips of paper which he saw were tickets for a concert.

"Cathryn Craig and Brian Willoughby are playing at the Slug & Lettuce in a couple of weeks' time. He's the Strawbs' guitarist isn't he? I recognised his name from your signed photo. I'll go with you."

He felt his eyes filling up at he thoughtfulness. "Thanks Ria, I'm really touched. That's a lovely idea. But wouldn't you rather be going somewhere with Kieran?"

She turned her face away from him before replying. "Kieran and I have broken up, Dad - he dumped me for some old slag who threw herself at him at one of his concerts. She'd moved into his flat within a week"

"Oh, Darling, I'm so sorry. When did that happen?"

"A couple of weeks ago" she replied and then collapsed in floods of tears.

"Why didn't you tell me? Does your mother know?"

"I've only told Matt. Mum is under so much pressure at work and your mind has obviously been on your… elsewhere. I'll be okay, it'll just take me a little while to get over the creep."

He took her hand and, for the first time in years, she did not pull it away.

"I know there's nothing worse than having crumblies like me telling you that it will pass and that you've got your whole life ahead of you, but its true. You will get over him, darling, and probably sooner than you think."

"I know Dad, but that doesn't, like, make it feel any easier right now."

"It will get easier, though, Ria-but don't worry, I'm not going to tell you that there are plenty more fish in the sea-I can remember deciding to throttle the next person who told me that."

"Were you ever dumped, then, Dad?"

"Of course I was-most memorably by your mother."

"By Mum? I thought it was love at first sight and all that."

"It was for me and I thought the feeling was vaguely mutual…until she ditched me for a character called Tarquin."

"Tarquin! What kind of name's that?"

"Tarquin Smith-Pembleton, to give him his full title. I'm sure the reason she insisted on hyphenating Cadogan and Troy was because she'd missed out on a double-barrelled name by not marrying Tarquin."

"So what happened to him?"

"I don't know-they fell out pretty quickly and your mother and I got back together again."

"Just think: otherwise, you might have been a Smith-Pembleton and been brought up in a stately pile in Berkshire."

"Sounds cool but I'm happy enough living in Islington with a Dad who's got a stately pile of Strawbs' records-and it was quite nice being called Helena at school."

"That's about the nicest thing you've ever said to me," he laughed. "But why Helena?"

"Helena Troy: like, Helen Of Troy-get it?"

227

"That's very classical and sophisticated-I had to put up with being called Doris when I was at school."

"That's not very cool, Dad."

"Truth to tell, Darling, I wasn't very cool anyway-at your age, I hadn't really even dated a girl, let alone snogged one."

"Seriously, Dad?"

"Never more so: there was a girl called Jane who I think wanted me to kiss her but all we ever did was talk about football."

"So this Sally was someone you, like, knew at Uni?"

"Yeah, we went out for a few months but...I guess I didn't treat her very kindly.

"It's strange" he mused. "Nowadays teenagers seem desperate to get into a serious 'relationship' and shack up with someone as soon as they can. In my day, that was the last thing any of us wanted-we just wanted to have lots of fun. My idea of taking Sally out on a date was dragging her down the Panton Arms with Pete and Roger.... Perhaps that's why she didn't exactly seem heartbroken when I ended it."

"It wasn't exactly, like, wine and roses with Kieran-we spent most of our time together at gigs."

"I must admit that I quite liked the guy-he was very complimentary about Strawbs."

"Confession time, Dad: when he first came round to the house, I told him that his best chance of making a good impression on you was to say nice things about your musical tastes-it obviously worked, then."

"You little minx-what tips did you give him for impressing your mother?"

"I told him that the only way that he might even get her to notice him was to tell her that his dad's, like, an important venture capitalist but I'm not sure they ever even spoke to each other."

He laughed. "I tell you what, next time you bring a boyfriend home, I'll tell you the buzzwords that your mother likes to hear in every sentence.... But take your time, Ria, have some fun with your friends and don't go rushing into another heavy scene."

"I won't, Dad, and I'm not going to get stressed-out over Kieran any more, I promise. But are you okay now?"

"Yes, thanks, Darling. The trouble with being reunited with old flames is that you get a glimpse of the life you might have had if things had worked out differently and it can completely turn your real life upside down…but I wouldn't swap you for anything in the world-or Matt or your mother for that matter."

They talked on for a long time - first of all about Kieran but then he began to tell her stories about his student days and his school days and began to realise that, behind all the painted-on maturity and teenage attitude, she was not really so different from the little girl of a few years previously who loved him to sit on her bed before kissing her goodnight and would listen, enthralled, while he hold her stories of magic carpets and treasure maps-how he used to wish that she could stay cocooned for ever in the safety of her room, with its fluffy rabbits and the teddy bear with one ear, where he could shield her from the harsh realities of life.

She'll be a forty-something with "what ifs" of her own before long, he thought sadly. I just hope she never feels she's wasted her opportunities - but she's got to lead her own life and to be free to make her own mistakes.

Eventually she left to do some college work, leaving Nigel to wonder how long it had been since he had had quality time like that with a member of his own family and to reflect on how enjoyable it had been.

Remembering the vow he had made earlier, he decided to go out to enjoy the autumn sun and to buy some Doris Troy CDs but before doing so he could not resist checking his e-mails one last time and was surprised to see an e-mail from a Debbie Jones, the subject of which just said *"Hi, Nigel"*.

To: *Nigel Troy*
From: *Debbie Jones*
Remember me? Dave Such's sister? Dave gave me your e-mail address.

I am living in London too - in Balham. I work for a firm of estate agents and am recently divorced (from Mr Jones, as you have probably guessed).

I remember you and I having a lovely evening out and then going onto a party where I ruined it all by getting off with Kevin Tolley - I still feel bad about that and wonder what would have happened if things had worked out differently that night. My fault for being sooooo naughty! Do you fancy a drink some time?

Love

Debbie

As he read it, Nigel became convulsed with laughter at the thought that he was now himself on the receiving end of a "what if" e-mail. There was also a delightful symmetry in the way that Debbie, the girl for whom he had ditched Sally, had tried to resurface in his life on the day on which Sally exited it for the second-and last-time.

There was only one thing to do, though - a reply which made it clear that he was not going down the same road as with Sally and which nipped in the bud any possible flirtation with Debbie- in the words of Thomas Hardy, he told himself, I will traverse old love's domain, never again.

To: Debbie Jones

From: Nigel Troy

Hello, Debbie, good to hear from you.

No need to feel bad about what happened 25 years ago - I always assumed that it was just that you were suffering from tonsillitis and that this Kevin's tongue had magical healing powers.

Or maybe that you were reading anthropology and concluded that he was worthy of close and in-depth study as the Missing Link between Neanderthal Man and whatever went before him.

Either way, Debbie, never, ever think "what if?" about anything. The future is bright-just look in your mailbox! The possibilities are limitless: breast enlargement, HRT, hunky East European and mysterious Orientals looking for meaningful relationships....

You can even see your favourite soap stars naked.

Your life is flying past, so seek out new avenues of pleasure-don't waste it trying to re-live your youth with me.

Regards

Nigel

I couldn't make myself any clearer he thought to himself, before adding

PS I was thinking of going to the Saatachi Gallery next Saturday morning....